Business Intelligence consulting group

Oracle BI Enterprise Edition

Dashboard & Report Design & Best Practices

Amy Mayer

Kevin McGinley

Cover design by Jeremiah Johnson
Book design by Dan Sack & Brian Ferin

Printed in the United States of America via Lulu Press (www.lulu.com)

First Printing: October 2008

ISBN-13: 978-0-615-26295-6

Publisher: BI Consulting Group LLC, 860 Blue Gentian Road, Suite 290, Eagan, MN 55121 – www.biconsultinggroup.com

Author's website: www.biconsultinggroup.com

Acknowledgements

This guide has been a work in progress for a number of years and will continue to be refined for years to come. As such, a number of different people have contributed ideas, words, and time to this guide and we feel compelled to acknowledge them, for without them, the guide wouldn't be what it is today.

Michael Martin brought his passion and ideas to help bring the guide to life. Brad Reinders contributed his best practice experiences to the guide and spent countless hours reviewing and re-reviewing it. Mike Jelen helped shape many of the original best practices and became the caretaker for the guide to make sure we were continuing to give it the attention it deserved. Brian Ferin and Dan Sack assumed the laborious and ungrateful task of making sure the guide was accurate, up-to-date, and looked fantastic.

We want to thank all of them for their hard work in making this guide something we're proud of.

Amy & Kevin

Table of Contents

Table of Contents

Table of Contents

Introduction

BI Consulting Group has developed what is recognized as the most complete, most comprehensive set of dashboard and report design "best practice" standards ever developed, specific to Oracle Business Intelligence (formerly Siebel Business Analytics).

These best practices have not been created simply to provide a "standard", instead they are based on the most important litmus test – what standards actually cause dashboards to be used, and what "best practices" of dashboard and report development provide insight into the business, rather than just reports.

This guide was started with the Siebel Analytics 7.8.x platform, before Oracle acquired Siebel. The current version of the guide reflects Oracle's 10.1.3.3.x releases of Oracle Business Intelligence Enterprise Edition (OBIEE). Expect this guide to be enhanced and revised with subsequent major releases of OBIEE.

Intended Audience

This guide is intended for Oracle BI dashboard designers, report designers and super users. In addition, business analysts and regular users may find this text useful as it will help them better understand the concepts behind their BI implementation and may give them ideas for future releases. The guide is not meant to serve as a "training" manual, but rather as a best practices reference. Therefore, it is advisable (although not required), that before reading this guide, you should have already completed a more formal introductory training or at least familiarized yourself with the Oracle BI environment. BI Consulting Group offers a wide range of Oracle BI training courses, and this guide is meant to serve as a supplement and additional reference material for these courses. For more information on the Oracle BI courses offered by BI Consulting Group, please visit http://www.bicguniversity.com.

Chapter Structure

The first chapter in this text introduces, at a high level, the guiding principles of dashboard design. The remaining chapters deal with the individual features and components that comprise the dashboard. Each chapter may contain multiple topics and each topic typically contains three main sections. In the first section, we introduce the topic in non-technical terms; provide some context; and in some cases provide examples and screenshots.

In the second section, aptly titled *Best Practices*, we formally define the best practices associated with the containing topic. As many best practices apply to more than one topic, we will formally define the best practice once and will then reference the best practice repeatedly in other chapters. Each best practice is identified using italic blue font as in Figure 0.1.

> ***BP 2.2:*** *All numeric views should utilize alternating row "green bar" styling for improved legibility unless there are other overriding style requirements.*
>
> Oracle BI offers a built-in feature called **alternating row "green bar" styling**, which formats alternating table rows using different colors. This coloring separates the data rows and makes the table more legible, especially when examining the column values in a data row from left to right. The table below illustrates this feature.

Figure 0.1 Example of a Best Practice

The indented paragraph below the best practice offers further explanation and examples when necessary. Like the first section, this second section, avoids using technical terminology for the most part, and instead focuses on explaining the concepts using general language.

The third section, titled *Quick Reference Instructions* (QRI for short), is where we have placed the majority of the detailed, step-by-step content and product-specific terminology. This section contains the "How-To's" for all of the non-basic tasks presented in or related to the previous two sections. Our intent here is to separate the conceptual content from the instructive so that you can easily find the information you need if you wish to use this guide for future reference (as is our hope). Each QRI section will start off by listing its contents in bulleted form, and will then provide step by step instructions in outline form for each "How-To", as in Figure 0.2. These are the three sections you will find for most topics.

This section contains instructions for the following topics:

- How to enable alternating row "green bar" styling
- How to set the pivot table width to 100%
- How to insert page breaks after each section
- How to add Totals to the pivot table

I. How to enable alternating row "green bar" styling

1. In the **Pivot Table View**, click the **Pivot Table View Properties** button
2. Check the **Enable alternating row "green bar" styling** checkbox
3. Click **OK**

II. How to set the pivot table width to 100%

1. In the **Pivot Table View**, click the **Content Properties** button

Figure 0.2 Example of Quick Reference Instructions

Chapter 1: Dashboard Design Primer

Oracle BI Enterprise Edition is a wonderfully flexible tool, allowing for dramatic creativity on dashboard design, but the fact is, without following a proven set of best practices, it is possible to create dashboards that are difficult to use and do not provide the insight and flexibility that the end user is looking for.

The dashboard best practices standards contained within this guide have been developed by BI Consulting Group after more than 280 implementations of Oracle Business Intelligence and its previous incarnations, Siebel Analytics and nQuire. These best practices have been adjusted and updated based upon each new release of the software, and based upon our own iterative methodology, which derives a large amount of user feedback from each implementation.

The Six Guiding Principles of Dashboard Design

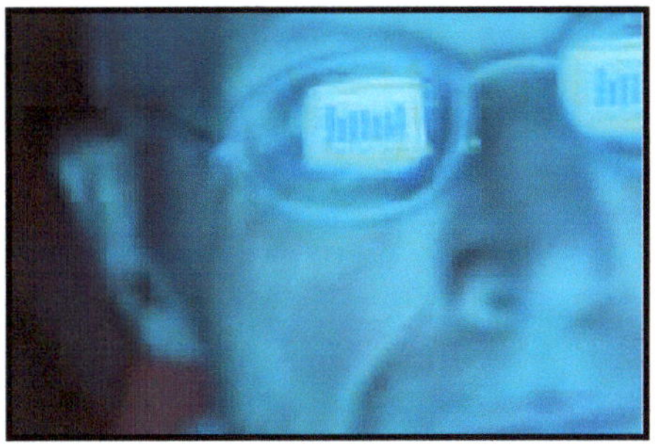

Most of the best practices standards we've provided, once learned, can be quickly implemented on each new dashboard created. Others will take some practice, but all have been proven in production implementations, each of which have received overwhelming user acceptance. Our advice is to avoid the approach of "getting something out the door" and then going back later to apply best practices; instead, we recommend using these standards and best practices from the very start with the first release. The fact is, once you've learned the ideas in this document (in particular our section on "Shortcuts, Cheats and Other Tips & Tricks"), you'll discover that you can build a powerful, flexible, and aesthetically pleasing report in the same time it takes to build a clumsy, static, low-functionality report.

This guide contains literally dozens of great best practices, each of which falls under at least one of the following six Tenets of Dashboard Design.

I. Provide insight, not reports.

When a key user drops off a stack of Excel spreadsheets in response to your request for "requirements", take the time to understand what results they are trying to derive from that content. Understand what they search for, what they mark up with a yellow highlighter, and what they look at next after discovering an exception. With the best practices that follow, you'll discover that you can offer multiple ways of providing insight from the same content packed into one Excel spreadsheet (which offered no insight, just data); and that you'll be able to compact multiple Excel spreadsheets into a single, flexible report module that can fit into the upper left hand corner of a dashboard. Column selectors, view selectors, and bubble charts are not complex. If you think they are, see Tenet #3.

II. Protect your real estate and eliminate the white space.

Unlike printed reports where you can get away with saying "the answer is on page 42", the same is not true for online dashboards where you will most likely be restricted to what you can fit into an 1024 x 768 pixel screen (or 1024 x 2304 if your dashboard is three pages long). If your users can't derive insight in the first few seconds of looking at a dashboard, the design could use improvement. If your dashboard has large patches of white space, it will look incomplete to the users and you are wasting space. If you believe that it's impossible to fit meaningful content into 1024 x 2304 pixels, go check out popular Internet portals like MyYahoo, Google, or MSN.

III. Trust your users will get it.

Most users in today's business world are familiar with browsing the web and the typical controls used to shop, bank, research, and consume information. Controls like dropdowns, buttons, checkboxes, and text fields are all used on popular sites throughout the Internet – and on OBIEE, too! Trust your users. If you've followed rules #1 and #2, your users are going to get it.

IV. Merge business skills into your IT skills.

In order to create the insightful reports we discussed in Tenet #1, report designers need to know more than what the business users are asking for on a report. A highly successful BI project will have designers who know the business side well and can develop new reports and enhance existing ones without explicit instruction from the business users. In Business Intelligence, we need to move away from simply asking what the user wants the report to look like and what data they want in the database. We need to move toward understanding the business processes and determining what data and reports will bring the insight the users need. Once you've gotten to know the processes driving the reports, you can make suggestions to the users on what they need to be successful. Most of your users have no idea what kind of reports Oracle BI is capable of producing when utilized to its full potential. With a time spent getting to better know the business, you'll be able to deliver powerful, insightful reports the users hadn't considered or didn't even know were possible.

V. Design your dashboard (and insight) in Oracle BI itself using an iterative methodology.

Dashboard design requires multiple iterations to be successful. Business users often don't know or realize what they want until they can see something they like or something they recognize needs to be changed. It's important that you have a plan in place during the build process that allows for several levels of refinement. This plan should include a sound strategy for capturing and documenting user input, prioritizing the changes, and determining the complexity. Careful planning of this process will ensure that all iterations run smoothly and add as much value as possible.

VI. Be prepared to review, refine, and re-do.

After you've rolled out your BI project, if the implementation is viewed as a success by the users, you'll notice that BI slowly becomes more pervasive throughout your organization and is eventually no longer thought of as BI - it's simply part of the way the business is run. But the business focus can change, processes change, needs change. A periodic review should be done to assess whether the dashboards are still meeting the needs of the business as well as when they were first deployed. Refinement may be needed to evolve the dashboards with the business, and sometimes even a more dramatic re-do is necessary.

Organizational Structure

Now that we have presented the Guiding Principles of Dashboard Design, we will quickly review the basic composition of the Oracle BI dashboard. Although the dashboard is typically the only presentation that is displayed to the end user, the dashboard design begins at a much more atomic level. While the dashboard is the end product, the initial starting point is an empty request. A "request" in Oracle BI is what most people would call a "report" in other applications. From this point on, we will usually use the term report, as it is the more commonly used term.

A designer builds a report in Oracle BI by first inserting the desired columns and then enabling different views and objects in the Compound Layout view. We use the term "view" to refer to any tables, pivot tables, charts and graphs. There are also other objects that could be considered views in their own right, but are perhaps better explained as "other report objects" or "other view objects". These objects would include column selectors, view selectors, legends, filters, and so on.

Views and view objects represent the most atomic level of design. As such, we believe it makes the most sense to begin with this bottom level and work our way up to the top. Therefore, the following chapters will first explore the individual views, then the other view objects, then the report, and finally the dashboard. As we move up this organizational hierarchy (i.e. views to reports to dashboards), notice how many of the best practices apply to more than one level of the hierarchy, and all of the best practices support one or more of the tenets provided in the previous section.

Chapter 2: Grid Views

In this text, the term "grid views" refers to both tables (tabular views), and pivot tables (sometimes referred to as cross-tabs) because they present data in a row/column grid, similar to a spreadsheet. Tables and pivot tables are similar in that they both focus on displaying data values, but they are different in their presentation of the data.

Grid views are extremely valuable in the following situations:

- The users need to see the detail behind a visual, such as a chart
- The users need to look at the lowest level of detail in the data
- The users want to analyze how multiple attributes interact

In this chapter, we will first discuss tables, the simpler of the two, and will then move on to pivot tables. Lastly, we will explain conditional formatting, which is a special feature that is commonly used with grid views.

Tabular Views

Most people are familiar with the concept of tables, as the tabular report is one of the easiest and most common ways to display data; however, most people may not be familiar with the best practices associated with designing a good tabular report. Many tabular reports accomplish the basic objective of simply displaying data, but where many designs fail is in providing actual insight and value in an efficient manner without requiring excessive analysis. A user should not have to sift through mountains of data to find a morsel of insight. The following best practices will help you design a tabular view that is useful, usable, and functional.

Best Practices

BP 2.1: Grid views should have their width set to 100%.

By default, numeric views do not take up 100% of the available width. Typically, a grid view will end up being displayed in a dashboard column, so it is important to set the width to 100% to eliminate white space in the dashboard. Setting the width to 100% will cause the table to expand to fit the width of the dashboard column in which it is placed. In addition, if the user exports the report to a PDF via the Print to PDF feature, the report will also stretch to 100% of the available PDF document.

Figure 2.1 demonstrates how tables should appear in dashboard columns if the table widths are set to 100%.

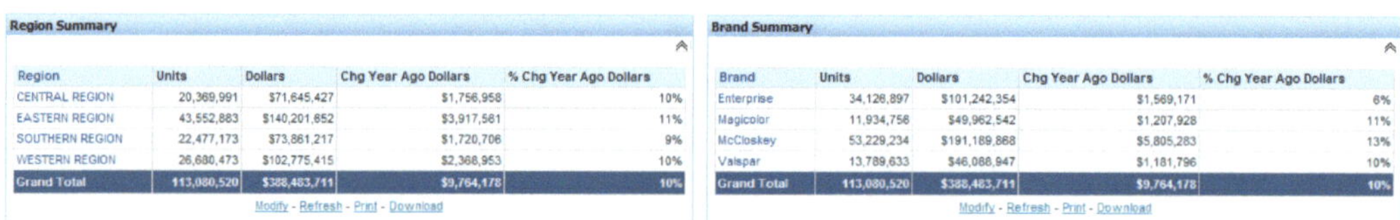

Figure 2.1 Dashboard displaying tables set to 100% width.

In contrast, Figure 2.2 demonstrates the default table appearance if the width is not explicitly set to 100%. Notice that the tables do not fill the available space in the containing columns. The result is a less finished, less polished look. Placing several table views on a dashboard that don't fill their space results in a dashboard that looks incomplete, which can distract users from focusing on the things they need to see.

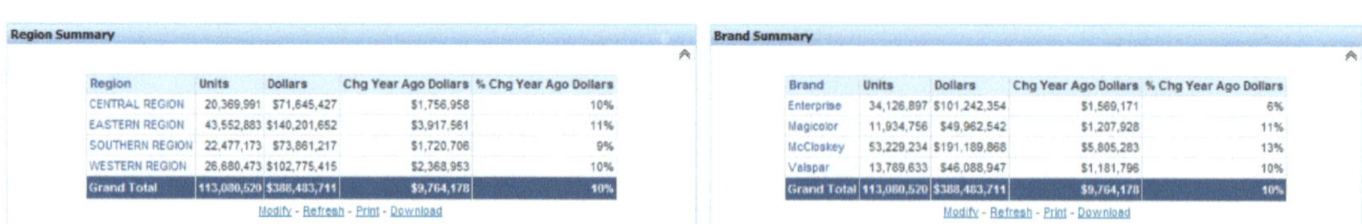

Figure 2.2 Dashboard displaying default appearance of tables with no width setting.

***BP 2.2:** Grid views should utilize alternating row "green bar" styling for improved legibility unless there are other overriding style requirements.*

Oracle BI offers a built-in feature called alternating row "green bar" styling, which formats alternating table rows using different colors. This coloring separates the data rows and makes the table more legible, especially when examining the column values in a data row from left to right. Figure 2.3 illustrates this feature.

Region	Units	Dollars	Chg Year Ago Dollars	% Chg Year Ago Dollars
CENTRAL REGION	20,369,991	$71,645,427	$1,756,958	10%
EASTERN REGION	43,552,883	$140,201,652	$3,917,561	11%
SOUTHERN REGION	22,477,173	$73,861,217	$1,720,706	9%
WESTERN REGION	26,680,473	$102,775,415	$2,368,953	10%
Grand Total	**113,080,520**	**$388,483,711**	**$9,764,178**	**10%**

Figure 2.3 Table illustrating alternating row "green bar" styling.

***BP 2.3:** When ordering columns in a tabular view, the parent attribute should always be located in the left-outer-most column followed by the respective children (if there are any) in hierarchical order. If it is preferable to stack parent and child attributes, creating a sort of tree diagram in the column headings, then a pivot table view should be used instead.*

For example, if a company uses a geographic hierarchy where regions are at the top level, districts are at the middle level, and markets are at the lowest level, then a report showing both the hierarchy and the market-level data should look like Figure 2.4.

Region	District	Market	Units	Dollars
CENTRAL REGION	CHICAGO DISTRICT	CHICAGO	5,625,844	$20,082,035
		MILWAUKEE	1,425,689	$5,121,150
	CINCINNATI DISTRICT	CINCINNATI	1,207,474	$4,232,015
		COLUMBUS	1,033,712	$3,528,277
		INDIANAPOLIS	1,918,644	$5,710,862
	DETROIT DISTRICT	DETROIT	4,804,170	$16,404,481
	KANSAS CITY DISTRICT	KANSAS CITY	983,583	$3,688,422
		OKLAHOMA CITY/TULSA	658,174	$2,389,214
		ST. LOUIS	1,395,504	$5,593,864
	MINNEAPOLIS DISTRICT	MINNEAPOLIS	1,317,197	$4,895,107
EASTERN REGION	BOSTON DISTRICT	BOSTON	8,587,711	$25,472,468
		HARTFORD/NEW HAVEN	2,750,338	$8,177,640
	NEW YORK DISTRICT	NEW YORK	14,329,748	$46,497,637
	PHILADELPHIA DISTRICT	PHILADELPHIA	9,501,902	$29,827,430
		WASHINGTON D.C.	2,617,159	$8,912,749
	YOUNGSTOWN DISTRICT	CLEVELAND	3,372,804	$12,429,258
		PITTSBURGH	2,393,221	$8,884,470

Figure 2.4 Table with hierarchical columns displayed left to right.

Alternately, if the preference is to stack the parent and child attributes, then the data should be displayed in a pivot table, as in Figure 2.5.

	CENTRAL REGION					EASTERN REGION		
	CHICAGO DISTRICT		CINCINNATI DISTRICT			NEW YORK DISTRICT	PHILADELPHIA DISTRICT	
	CHICAGO	MILWAUKEE	CINCINNATI	COLUMBUS	INDIANAPOLIS	NEW YORK	PHILADELPHIA	WASHINGTON D.C.
Units	5,625,844	1,425,689	1,207,474	1,033,712	1,918,644	14,329,748	9,501,902	2,617,159
Dollars	$20,082,035	$5,121,150	$4,232,015	$3,528,277	$5,710,862	$46,497,637	$29,827,430	$8,912,749

Figure 2.5 Pivot Table with stacked parent and child attributes.

BP 2.4: *Tabular views should have a grand total row at the bottom of the view, unless grand totals do not make sense for the particular data.*

A user benefits from the grand total row by being able to see a second, higher level of information without taking any other action on the report. The totals in the grand total row can be calculated using different aggregate functions. The grand total calculation for each column is based on the default aggregation type for that column. It is possible to override a column's aggregate function for a specific report and even set a specific column to display no grand total at all (common on a report that shows product prices). Figure 2.6 demonstrates the grand total row that should be used as a common practice.

Region	Units	Dollars	Year Ago Dollars	% Chg Year Ago Dollars
CENTRAL REGION	20,369,991	$71,645,427	$64,932,184	10%
EASTERN REGION	43,552,883	$140,201,652	$126,453,540	11%
SOUTHERN REGION	22,477,173	$73,861,217	$67,497,528	9%
WESTERN REGION	26,680,473	$102,775,415	$93,279,601	10%
Grand Total	113,080,520	$388,483,711	$352,162,853	10%

Figure 2.6 Table displaying a grand total row.

BP 2.5: Tables displaying grand total rows should be set to display "Report-Based Totals".

If left unchecked, the table view defaults to a grand total (totaling the entire result set, rather than totaling the filtered items that are on the report itself).

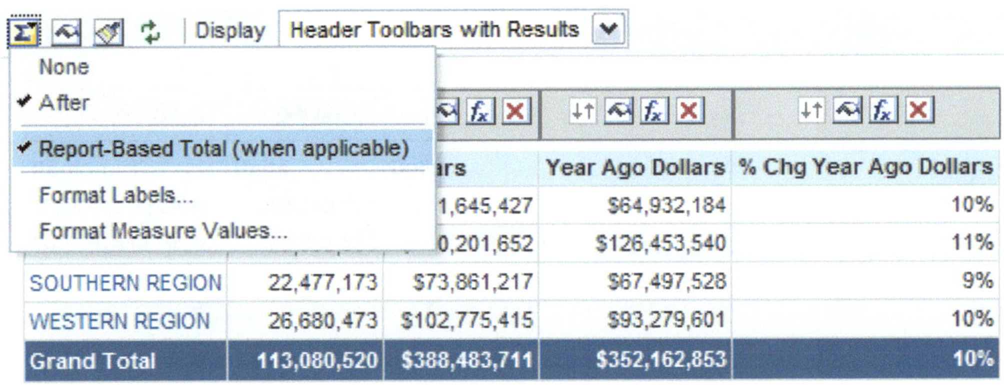

Figure 2.7 Screenshot showing where to set the Report-Based Total option.

BP 2.6: Column sorting on a dashboard should be enabled for table views unless a specific sort is required for a report.

BP 2.7: Paging controls should be displayed at the bottom of each table.

BP 2.8: To enhance the overall presentation of a tabular report, both column headings and table headings should be displayed (as separate rows) and should be formatted individually using colors and borders.

When creating a report in OBI Answers, the Pick List on the left side of the screen shows the columns that can be included in the report. These columns are grouped under logical headings such as "Periods" or "Sales Measures". In Answers, these headings are referred to as table headings and the column names underneath them are referred to as column headings.

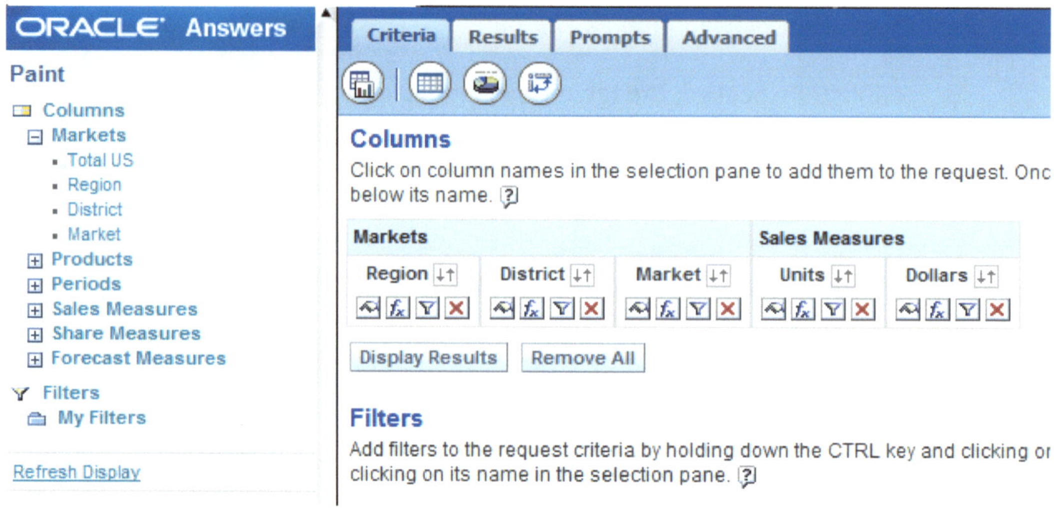

Figure 2.8 The Pick List and the Criteria Tab both show table headings and column headings.

In the Table Properties, there is an option to display both the column and table headings as separate rows. Selecting this option will cause the table to display two header rows as seen in Figure 2.9; there's a top row for the table heading and a second row for the column heading.

Markets	Periods	Sales Measures			
Region	Year	Units	Dollars	Year Ago Dollars	% Chg Year Ago Dollars
CENTRAL REGION	2006	10,769,039	$38,316,684	$26,615,500	44.0% ▲
CENTRAL REGION	2007	1,756,958	$6,713,243	$38,316,684	-82.5% ▼
EASTERN REGION	2006	24,943,553	$80,360,001	$46,093,539	74.3% ▲
EASTERN REGION	2007	3,917,561	$13,748,112	$80,360,001	-82.9% ▼
SOUTHERN REGION	2006	12,099,546	$39,586,439	$27,911,089	41.8% ▲
SOUTHERN REGION	2007	1,720,706	$6,363,689	$39,586,439	-83.9% ▼
WESTERN REGION	2006	14,681,590	$56,479,644	$36,799,957	53.5% ▲
WESTERN REGION	2007	2,368,953	$9,495,814	$56,479,644	-83.2% ▼
Grand Total		72,257,906	$251,063,626	$352,162,853	-28.7%

Figure 2.9 Column headings and table headings displayed as separate rows.

In addition to displaying both of these headings, you have the option to rename or rearrange them. If the metadata repository is well designed and well labeled, then the column headings are usually descriptive and user-friendly as is, but often times the table headings could benefit from being renamed or rearranged. Renaming the table headings gives the report designer the opportunity to group like attributes and metrics under different table headings.

For example, in Figure 2.9, instead of using the existing table heading "Sales Measures", it might make more sense in this report to split this into two table headings – one called "This Year" and one called "Last Year". Underneath "This Year" would be the "Units" and "Dollars". Underneath "Last Year" would be "Year Ago Dollars" and "% Chg Year Ago Dollars".

After renaming and rearranging the headings, the next step would be to add colors and borders to the headings. The final result is a highly formatted tabular report as seen in Figure 2.10, which immediately draws the user's eyes to the logical column groupings.

Markets	Periods	This Year		Last Year	
Region	Year	Units	Dollars	Year Ago Dollars	% Chg Year Ago Dollars
CENTRAL REGION	2006	10,769,039	$38,316,684	$26,615,500	44.0% ▲
CENTRAL REGION	2007	1,756,958	$6,713,243	$38,316,684	-82.5% ▼
EASTERN REGION	2006	24,943,553	$80,360,001	$46,093,539	74.3% ▲
EASTERN REGION	2007	3,917,561	$13,748,112	$80,360,001	-82.9% ▼
SOUTHERN REGION	2006	12,099,546	$39,586,439	$27,911,089	41.8% ▲
SOUTHERN REGION	2007	1,720,706	$6,363,689	$39,586,439	-83.9% ▼
WESTERN REGION	2006	14,681,590	$56,479,644	$36,799,957	53.5% ▲
WESTERN REGION	2007	2,368,953	$9,495,814	$56,479,644	-83.2% ▼
Grand Total		72,257,906	$251,063,626	$352,162,853	-28.7%

Figure 2.10 Table with formatted table headings and column headings.

Quick Reference Instructions

This section contains instructions for the following topics:

- How to modify the table view (using best practice settings)
    a. How to set the Paging Controls
    b. How to set the Rows per Page
    c. How to Display Column & Table Headings as separate rows

   d. How to enable alternating row "green bar" styling
   e. How to enable column sorting in dashboards

- How to set the table width to 100%
- How to rename and format column and table headings
- How to add a grand total row to the bottom of the table

I. How to modify the table view (using Best Practice settings)

1. In the **Table View**, click the **Table View Properties** button
2. In the **Paging Controls** drop-down menu, make sure **Bottom** is selected
3. In the **Rows per Page** text box, enter the number of rows to display per page; leave this box empty to display all table rows on the same page
4. In the **Display Column & Table Headings** drop-down menu, select **As separate rows**
5. Check the **Enable alternating row "green bar" styling** checkbox
6. Check the **Enable column sorting in Dashboards** checkbox
7. Click **OK**
8. How to set the table width to 100%
9. In the **Table View**, click the **Table View Properties** button
10. Click the plus sign to expand the **Additional Formatting Options**
11. Enter **100%** in the text box next to **Width**
12. Click **OK**

II. How to rename and format column and table headings

1. In the **Table View,** click the **Column Properties** button of the column whose headings will be changed
2. Go to the **Column Format** tab
3. Check the **Custom Headings** check box
4. In the **Table Heading** text box, enter a new Table Heading
5. Click the button to the right of the **Table Heading** text box (the icon with two A's on it)
6. In the **Edit Format** dialog box, specify any desired format settings for the Table Heading and click **OK**
7. In the **Column Heading** text box, enter a new Column Heading
8. Click the button to the right of the **Column Heading** text box (button has two A's on it)
9. In the **Edit Format** dialog box, specify any desired format settings for the Column Heading and click **OK**

10. In the **Edit Column Format** dialog box, click **OK**
11. Repeat steps 1-10 for any additional columns whose headings need to be changed

Note: There is a formatting shortcut when dealing with multiple columns that have the same table heading. If consecutive columns have the same table heading, then you only need to reformat the table heading one time, and the format will automatically be applied across all columns that share that table heading. For example, in Figure 2.11, the **Last Year** table heading only needed to be reformatted one time, and since the last two columns share this same table heading, the new format was automatically applied across both of these consecutive columns.

Markets	Periods	This Year		Last Year	
Region	Year	Units	Dollars	Year Ago Dollars	% Chg Year Ago Dollars
CENTRAL REGION	2006	10,769,039	$38,316,684	$26,615,500	44.0% ▲
CENTRAL REGION	2007	1,756,958	$6,713,243	$38,316,684	-82.5% ▼
EASTERN REGION	2006	24,943,553	$80,360,001	$46,093,539	74.3% ▲
EASTERN REGION	2007	3,917,561	$13,748,112	$80,360,001	-82.9% ▼
SOUTHERN REGION	2006	12,099,546	$39,586,439	$27,911,089	41.8% ▲
SOUTHERN REGION	2007	1,720,706	$6,363,689	$39,586,439	-83.9% ▼
WESTERN REGION	2006	14,681,590	$56,479,644	$36,799,957	53.5% ▲
WESTERN REGION	2007	2,368,953	$9,495,814	$56,479,644	-83.2% ▼
Grand Total		72,257,906	$251,063,626	$352,162,853	-28.7%

Figure 2.11 Table headings "This Year" and "Last Year" each apply to more than one column.

III. <u>How to add a grand total row to the bottom of the table</u>

1. In the **Table View**, click the **Grand Total** button
2. In the **Grand Total** drop-down menu, select **After**

Pivot Table Views

Pivot tables are similar to regular tables, but they offer additional flexibility and functionality. Many of the best practices discussed for regular tabular views also apply to pivot tables. These shared best practices will be restated later in this section, but first, we explain a few special features that make pivot tables so powerful.

Alternate Data Representations

Oracle BI provides a pivot table feature that allows you to quickly convert quantitative metrics into "percent of" or "index of" calculations. For example, instead of displaying a quantity such as a dollar amount or a number of units, the pivot table can be configured to express the quantity in terms of its percentage relative to the other values within its row, column, or other page element.

Figure 2.12 demonstrates how to express the "Dollars" metric in terms of its percentage relative to the other values in the same row.

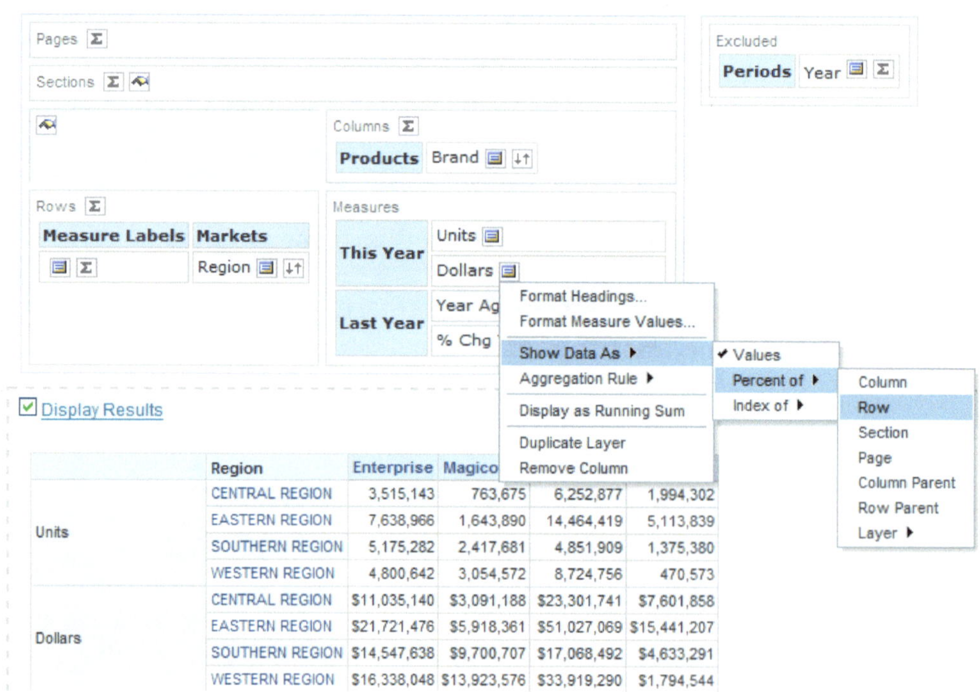

Figure 2.12 Settings to express the "Dollars" column as a Percent of Row.

In business terms, the "Dollars" metric will be changed to represent the percent to total across all brands within the region. The result is the new metric in Figure 2.13 (notice that we have also renamed the "Dollars" column to "Share of Dollars").

	Region	Enterprise	Magicolor	McCloskey	Valspar	Grand Total
Share of Dollars	CENTRAL REGION	24.5%	6.9%	51.7%	16.9%	100.0%
	EASTERN REGION	23.1%	6.3%	54.2%	16.4%	100.0%
	SOUTHERN REGION	31.7%	21.1%	37.1%	10.1%	100.0%
	WESTERN REGION	24.8%	21.1%	51.4%	2.7%	100.0%

Figure 2.13 Table showing the "Share of Dollars" column as a "Percent of" Row.

The original column can still be displayed in addition to the percent to total column, if desired. Oracle BI has a Duplicate Layer option, which can be used to create a copy of any metric in the pivot table. The copy can then be converted to a "percent to total" metric, leaving the original metric to be displayed alongside the new metric.

Re-pivoting

Have you ever been frustrated that you cannot re-pivot a pivot table from within a dashboard? We have invented a simple method to mimic re-pivoting by using column selectors to replace attributes in the rows, columns and/or sections. For example, in Figure 2.14, two column selectors have been added to the report with the labels "Rows:" (which would allow the replacement of the Region column) and "Columns:" (which would allow the replacement of the Year column).

You will notice in the "Columns" drop-down that you are not limited to simply swapping the attributes around (we can do more than just replace regions with years, and years with regions), you can add in additional attributes to be swapped into the pivot. Furthermore, you are not limited to replacing attributes from within the same dimension – notice that the user can change columns from Year to Month, as well as to District or Brand.

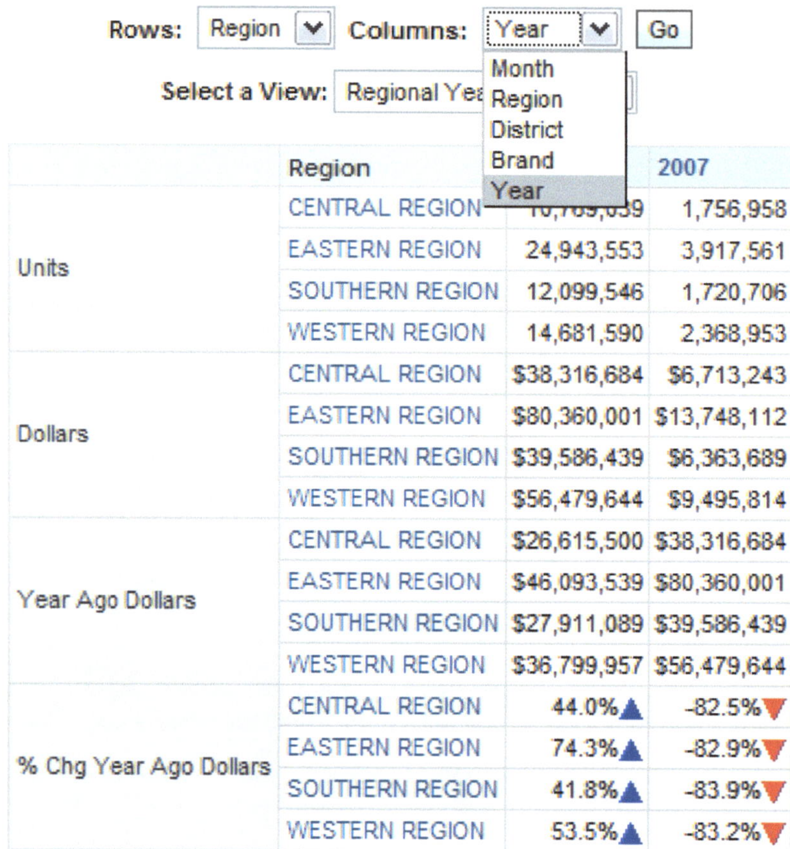

Figure 2.14 Re-pivoting using column selectors.

Breaking Data into Smaller "Chunks"

Pivot tables have the benefit of having a section within the editor that excludes any unwanted attributes or metrics that are displayed in other views of the containing report. This allows multiple pivot tables to be contained within the same report definition (unlike tabular views, which are more limited, in that all tabular views within the same report must display the same columns).

A view selector would allow the user to flip views between two or more pivot tables, allowing what might have been a very wide pivot table to be broken into manageable "chunks" of insight. In Figure 2.15, the user is interested in looking at dollars and units for this year and last year, also showing a difference and a percent change, which accounts for eight separate metrics. Rather than building a pivot table with eight metrics, the designer has broken the metrics into two logical chunks of four metrics for dollars and four metrics for units. Two separate pivot tables were created, and are made accessible to the user via a view selector.

Select a View: Dollars, This Year and Last Year

Year	Region	Dollars	Year Ago Dollars	Chg Year Ago Dollars	% Chg Year Ago Dollars
2006	CENTRAL REGION	$38,316,684	$26,615,500	$2,925,045	44.0%▲
	EASTERN REGION	$80,360,001	$46,093,539	$10,251,784	74.3%▲
	SOUTHERN REGION	$39,586,439	$27,911,089	$3,442,625	41.8%▲
	WESTERN REGION	$56,479,644	$36,799,957	$5,051,660	53.5%▲
2007	CENTRAL REGION	$6,713,243	$38,316,684	($9,012,081)	-82.5%▼
	EASTERN REGION	$13,748,112	$80,360,001	($21,025,992)	-82.9%▼
	SOUTHERN REGION	$6,363,689	$39,586,439	($10,378,840)	-83.9%▼
	WESTERN REGION	$9,495,814	$56,479,644	($12,312,637)	-83.2%▼

Figure 2.15 Pivot table "chunk" showing dollar metrics.

Selecting the alternate view would flip the user from dollars, as in Figure 2.15, to units, as in Figure 2.16:

Select a View: Units, This Year and Last Year

Year	Region	Units	Year Ago Units	Chg Year Ago Units	% Chg Year Ago Units
2006	CENTRAL REGION	10,769,039	7,843,994	2,925,045	37.3%▲
	EASTERN REGION	24,943,553	14,691,769	10,251,784	69.8%▲
	SOUTHERN REGION	12,099,546	8,656,921	3,442,625	39.8%▲
	WESTERN REGION	14,681,590	9,629,930	5,051,660	52.5%▲
2007	CENTRAL REGION	1,756,958	10,769,039	-9,012,081	-83.7%▼
	EASTERN REGION	3,917,561	24,943,553	-21,025,992	-84.3%▼
	SOUTHERN REGION	1,720,706	12,099,546	-10,378,840	-85.8%▼
	WESTERN REGION	2,368,953	14,681,590	-12,312,637	-83.9%▼

Figure 2.16 Pivot table "chunk" showing unit metrics.

Best Practices

Now that you are familiar with some of the features that make pivot tables special, we will discuss the best practices. The following best practices have already been stated in the section on tabular views, but are restated here as they also apply to pivot tables:

> ***BP 2.1**: Grid views should have their width set to 100%.*
>
> ***BP 2.2:** Grid views should utilize alternating row "green bar" styling for improved legibility unless there are other overriding style requirements.*

The remainder of this section discusses best practices that apply only to pivot tables.

***BP 2.9:** Pivot tables should have a Grand Total row at the bottom of the view and subtotal rows placed after the detailed line items, unless Grand Totals or subtotals do not make sense for the particular data.*

Figure 2.17 demonstrates subtotals and Grand Totals.

		2005	2006	2007
Region	**District**	**Dollars**	**Dollars**	**Dollars**
CENTRAL REGION	CHICAGO DISTRICT	$9,893,875	$12,945,705	$2,363,605
	CINCINNATI DISTRICT	$4,291,464	$7,800,295	$1,379,395
	DETROIT DISTRICT	$6,385,475	$8,524,076	$1,494,930
	KANSAS CITY DISTRICT	$4,108,605	$6,432,032	$1,130,863
	MINNEAPOLIS DISTRICT	$1,936,081	$2,614,576	$344,450
CENTRAL REGION Total		**$26,615,500**	**$38,316,684**	**$6,713,243**
EASTERN REGION	BOSTON DISTRICT	$12,721,254	$17,964,053	$2,964,801
	NEW YORK DISTRICT	$12,542,321	$29,328,594	$4,626,722
	PHILADELPHIA DISTRICT	$12,298,672	$22,206,245	$4,235,262
	YOUNGSTOWN DISTRICT	$8,531,292	$10,861,109	$1,921,327
EASTERN REGION Total		**$46,093,539**	**$80,360,001**	**$13,748,112**
SOUTHERN REGION	ATLANTA DISTRICT	$3,869,398	$5,760,758	$938,586
	CHARLOTTE DISTRICT	$1,292,535	$2,415,222	$349,864
	DALLAS DISTRICT	$7,839,032	$9,639,882	$1,681,740
	JACKSONVILLE DISTRICT	$12,760,789	$17,784,255	$2,694,325
	MEMPHIS DISTRICT	$2,149,335	$3,986,322	$699,174
SOUTHERN REGION Total		**$27,911,089**	**$39,586,439**	**$6,363,689**
WESTERN REGION	DENVER DISTRICT	$5,066,811	$7,006,656	$1,366,204
	LOS ANGELES DISTRICT	$19,598,510	$31,023,376	$5,485,609
	PORTLAND DISTRICT	$6,603,345	$9,570,740	$1,435,150
	SAN FRANCISCO DISTRICT	$5,531,291	$8,878,872	$1,208,851
WESTERN REGION Total		**$36,799,957**	**$56,479,644**	**$9,495,814**
Grand Total		**$137,420,085**	**$214,742,768**	**$36,320,858**

Figure 2.17 Pivot table displaying totals and subtotals.

***BP 2.10:** If a report has a pivot table with drillable elements, then the report should make the pivot table available through a view selector that also contains a tabular view.*

Keep in mind that most or all reports will be drillable, so when using a pivot table that has drillable elements in the columns, a best practice is to add a tabular view using a view selector. Since pivot tables will always show the entire data set at once, this allows users to switch to the tabular view and use page controls in the event that drilling down in the pivot table causes an enormous amount of records to be returned.

***BP 2.11**: If a pivot table is split into sections, page breaks should be inserted after each section.*

When designing a pivot table, one or more columns can be used to divide the results into sections. Page breaks should be inserted after each section by changing the "Insert Page Break" option in the Section Properties. The page breaks do not affect the way the pivot table is displayed on a dashboard (all of the sections will appear on the same page); however, page breaks do affect the way the pivot table appears when saved as a PDF. Figure 2.18 shows a pivot table PDF with no page breaks. In this example, the Region column is used to divide the data into sections.

CENTRAL REGION

	Enterprise	Magicolor	McCloskey	Valspar	Grand Total
Units	3,240,878	643,182	5,217,034	1,667,945	**10,769,039**
Dollars	$10,076,761	$2,595,426	$19,249,707	$6,394,790	**$38,316,684**
Year Ago Dollars	$6,743,753	$1,098,814	$13,413,251	$5,359,682	**$26,615,500**
% Chg Year Ago Dollars	49%	136%	44%	19%	**44%**

EASTERN REGION

	Enterprise	Magicolor	McCloskey	Valspar	Grand Total
Units	7,095,090	1,359,034	12,027,793	4,461,636	**24,943,553**
Dollars	$20,088,408	$4,859,985	$42,134,873	$13,276,735	**$80,360,001**
Year Ago Dollars	$11,910,399	$2,645,397	$25,138,712	$6,399,031	**$46,093,539**
% Chg Year Ago Dollars	69%	84%	68%	107%	**74%**

SOUTHERN REGION

	Enterprise	Magicolor	McCloskey	Valspar	Grand Total
Units	4,824,039	2,036,727	4,028,576	1,210,204	**12,099,546**
Dollars	$13,366,906	$8,153,238	$14,057,961	$4,008,334	**$39,586,439**
Year Ago Dollars	$9,564,380	$5,912,114	$9,176,284	$3,258,311	**$27,911,089**
% Chg Year Ago Dollars	40%	38%	53%	23%	**42%**

WESTERN REGION

	Enterprise	Magicolor	McCloskey	Valspar	Grand Total
Units	4,400,855	2,632,947	7,215,275	432,513	**14,681,590**
Dollars	$14,722,246	$12,047,837	$28,077,508	$1,632,053	**$56,479,644**
Year Ago Dollars	$9,381,520	$7,672,385	$18,145,029	$1,601,023	**$36,799,957**
% Chg Year Ago Dollars	57%	57%	55%	2%	**53%**

Figure 2.18 PDF version of a pivot table with no page breaks.

Figure 2.19 shows the same table with page breaks inserted after each section. Note that the PDF has 4 pages, one for each section/region (only the first page is shown below).

CENTRAL REGION

	Enterprise	Magicolor	McCloskey	Valspar	Grand Total
Units	3,240,878	643,182	5,217,034	1,667,945	**10,769,039**
Dollars	$10,076,761	$2,595,426	$19,249,707	$6,394,790	**$38,316,684**
Year Ago Dollars	$6,743,753	$1,098,814	$13,413,251	$5,359,682	**$26,615,500**
% Chg Year Ago Dollars	49%	136%	44%	19%	**44%**

Figure 2.19 PDF version of a pivot table with page breaks.

Quick Reference Instructions

This section contains instructions for the following topics:

- How to enable alternating row "green bar" styling
- How to set the pivot table width to 100%
- How to insert page breaks after each section
- How to add Totals to the pivot table

I. How to enable alternating row "green bar" styling

1. In the **Pivot Table View**, click the **Pivot Table View Properties** button
2. Check the **Enable alternating row "green bar" styling** checkbox
3. Click **OK**

II. How to set the pivot table width to 100%

1. In the **Pivot Table View**, click the **Content Properties** button
2. Click the plus sign to expand the **Additional Formatting Options**
3. Enter **100%** in the text box next to **Width**
4. Click **OK**

III. How to insert page breaks after each section

1. In the **Pivot Table View**, click the **Section Properties** button
2. In the **Insert Page Break** drop-down menu, select the column that should be used to determine where the page breaks are inserted. If you have placed any columns in the **Sections** page element of the **Pivot Table View**, those columns will appear in the **Insert Page Break** drop-down menu.
3. Click **OK**

IV. How to add totals to the pivot table

1. In the **Pivot Table View,** the each of the following page elements have their own **Totals** button (the button with a "Σ" on it):
    i. **Pages**
    ii. **Sections**
    iii. **Columns**
    iv. **Rows**
2. Totals can be applied to any of these page elements. To do so, click the **Totals** button in the page elements to which totals should be applied.
3. In the **Totals** drop-down menu, select **Before** or **After** to indicate where the totals should be displayed in relation to the other values in the page element.

Conditional Formatting

Conditional formatting is a feature that allows users to create reports where data values within the same column can be formatted differently based on a specified set of logical conditions. This feature is very useful for highlighting different user-defined conditions within a dataset. In addition to creating different formats for the text itself, Oracle BI also allows users to display different images as part of the conditional format. Users can reference custom images already uploaded to the server, or can choose from a predefined library of images.

It is important to note that conditional images are primarily targeted towards tabular and pivot table reports, and pivot table reports will only display the conditional image when the image is being displayed in the same column that is used in the "condition". For example, in the report below, the user could have chosen to put the up and down arrow in the "Region" column, but base that condition on the "% Chg Year Ago Dollars" column. That display would work in the tabular layout, but would not work in a pivot table.

Best Practices

BP 2.12: *Up or down arrow images should be included for columns that contain "+/-" data, percent change data, or percent comparison data. The images used should infer a direction in the shape, and not rely simply on color (such as stoplight bulbs) in the event the report is printed in black/white or grey tones.*

For example, Figure 2.20 contains up and down arrows as a conditional format for the "% Change Month Ago Dollars" column.

District	Units	Dollars	Chg Month Ago Dollars	% Chg Month Ago Dollars
MINNEAPOLIS DISTRICT	100,325	$379,268	$54,313.00	16.7% ▲
KANSAS CITY DISTRICT	161,761	$644,062	$35,759.00	5.9% ▲
CHICAGO DISTRICT	503,006	$1,736,998	($23,143.00)	-1.3% ▼
DETROIT DISTRICT	342,237	$1,161,946	($16,912.00)	-1.4% ▼
CINCINNATI DISTRICT	241,591	$759,910	($11,704.00)	-1.5% ▼
Grand Total	**1,348,920**	**$4,682,184**	**$753,697.00**	**16.2%**

Figure 2.20 Percent change data displayed using conditional formatting.

BP 2.13: *The standard when using images is that the image should be placed to the right of the data value if the column is numeric and to the left of the data value if the column is text.*

These are the default settings, because these settings ensure that the images are always in alignment vertically, regardless of the number of characters in each data value.

BP 2.14: *When using images in the conditional format, use a "blank" image as a placeholder for the case where none of the other specified conditions are met.*

Within most of the image families in the predefined library, there is a "blank" image, which is essentially just a transparent square the same size as the other images in the family. If you are using conditional formatting with images, and your set of conditions could potentially exclude certain data values, you need to add a final "catch all" condition that utilizes the blank image. The "catch all" condition should contain logic to capture any values left out of the other conditions.

Quick Reference Instructions

This section contains instructions for the following topic:

I. How to add conditional formats containing images

1. In the **Criteria** tab, open the **Column Properties** of the column to which the conditional format will be applied
2. Go to the **Conditional Format** tab
3. Click on **Add Condition**
4. Select the column that will be used within the logic of the condition
5. Specify the logic for the condition and click **OK**
6. In the **Edit Format** dialog box, click on the white box next to the word **Image**
7. Upload a custom image or select an image from the predefined library and click **OK**
8. In the **Edit Format** dialog box, specify any other desired settings and click **OK**
9. Repeat steps 3-8 for any additional conditions you wish to apply to this column

Chapter 3: Charts

Charting data is a great way to quickly provide a user with insight, rather than asking them to scroll through row after row or column after column of data, looking for trends and patterns with a fine tooth comb. But the fact is, most report designers run out of steam when they get past the basic pie, line or bar chart. The best practices below are meant to not only help the designer decide when one chart type might be more appropriate than another, but also to establish a proven set of chart standards. After covering some of the basic charting principles, we'll provide information on lesser known chart types such as scatter and bubble charts. While these charts might require some additional explanation to the end user, that time is well worth it. These chart types have been designed to maximize the amount of information (and insight) that the user can derive from the data, in as short a time as possible. They are also meant to uncover weaker data points that might typically be hidden by stronger data points.

General Charting Basics

Using charts to display data can be very valuable when comparing complex or aggregated measures. Even the most basic of charts can also be much more helpful than tabular reports when attempting to discover trends and patterns within the metrics being examined. There are a number of different types of charts available to you within Oracle BI, but choosing the right chart is only the first step towards constructing a dashboard that is powerful and insightful as well as aesthetically pleasing. In this first section, we've highlighted some of the best practices we've identified that can be applied to any type of chart.

Best Practices

BP 3.1: *When including a legend within any charted report, place the legend above the chart data.*

This will allow the user to see the legend more clearly and will also ensure that the user isn't required to scroll down to locate a hidden legend. Our eyes naturally scan from top to bottom, so the legend will be the first thing a user sees, making the chart colors more understandable. It will also help to make the chart wider and easier to read. The default settings in Oracle BI will place the legend on the right side of the chart. An exception to this is when only one metric is being charted, for instance in a vertical bar chart showing units by region, there will be no legend displayed by default. If the legend is to be omitted, the report title or the axis labels should clearly describe the attributes being charted. Figure 3.1 shows a bubble chart with the legend repositioned to the top of the report.

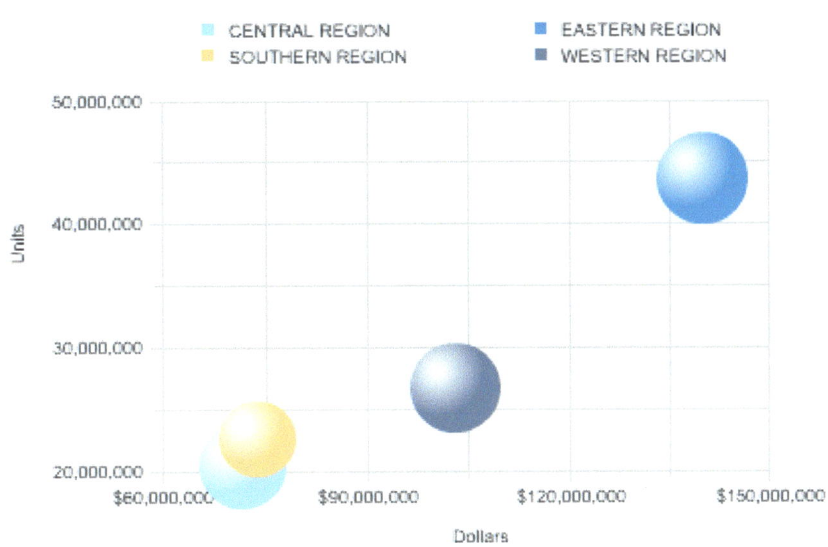

Figure 3.1 Bubble chart with legend placed above data.

BP 3.2: Data labels within charts should be shown if they can easily be read when displayed simultaneously. Otherwise, they should be shown only on rollover.

A good rule of thumb is to set the "Show data labels" option to "Default (On Rollover)" if more than six pie wedges or ten bars are being displayed. This option will hide all data labels, but will allow the users to view individual figures by hovering over a particular bar or wedge with their mouse cursor. Consider a pie chart splitting up individual markets across the entire U.S. In this case, setting this option to "Always" would likely cause figures to overlap and result in the chart being impossible to read. Figure 3.2 displays an example of a pie chart with four wedges that has the "Show data labels" option set to "Always".

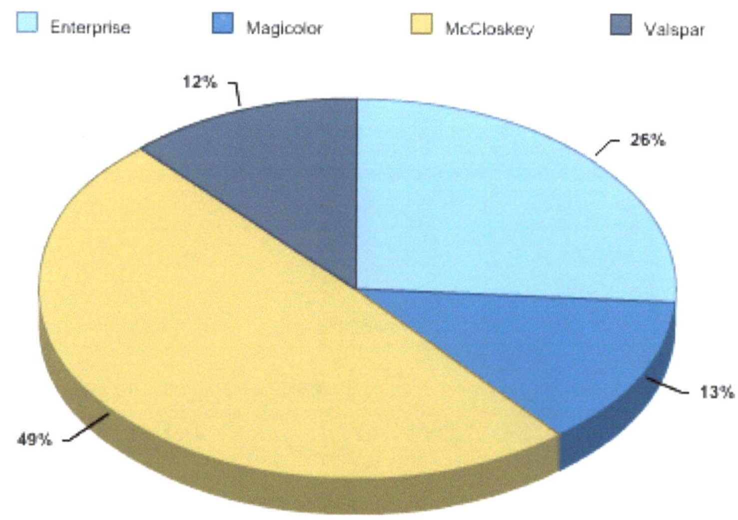

Figure 3.2 Pie chart with data labels set to always be displayed.

If this setting were changed to "On Rollover", then the resulting chart would resemble Figure 3.3. Data will only be displayed for the one bar or wedge over which the mouse is hovering.

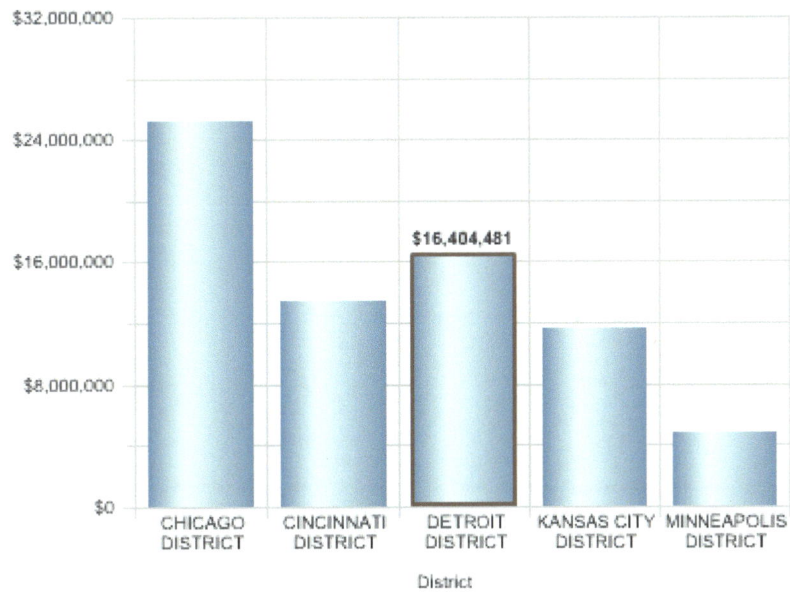

Figure 3.3 Bar chart with data labels set to only be shown on rollover.

***BP 3.3**: When a report containing a chart is likely to be printed, and data labels are displayed on rollover, a tabular or pivot table view should be made available by placing it beneath the chart view within the report.*

Users viewing printouts of reports will obviously not have the luxury of being able to hover over particular sections to view specific data labels. Displaying a corresponding table or pivot table ensures that the necessary figures are transferred to the printed report. Figure 3.4 shows how a tabular view can be added below a chart to assist users in interpreting the data.

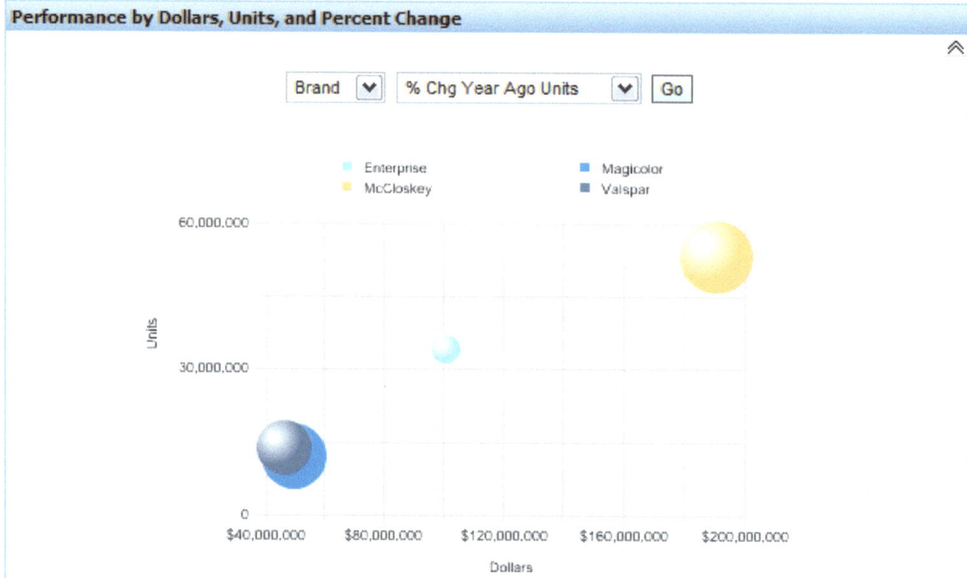

Brand	Units	Dollars	% Chg Year Ago Units
Enterprise	34,126,897	$101,242,354	5%
Magicolor	11,934,756	$49,962,542	11%
McCloskey	53,229,234	$191,189,868	12%
Valspar	13,789,633	$46,088,947	9%

Modify - Refresh - Print - Download

Figure 3.4 Bubble chart report with tabular data added below.

BP 3.4: *The same colors, background colors, and fonts should be used when designing any chart view. These can be the defaults in OBIEE or other standards defined by a company.*

When designing a particular chart within Answers, you should remember the fact that most reports will ultimately end up being displayed in a dashboard with a number of other tables and charts. Although a report may seem more pleasing to the eye with a new color scheme or title font when viewed independently, a dashboard page full of reports with differing colors and fonts will look unprofessional and may prove to be distracting to the user. A dashboard should always have a clean, consistent look. Using the same colors and fonts for all reports will also ensure that reports can easily be moved between dashboards or pages without worrying about presentation. The most common exception to this would be altering the color series of a chart when trying to "call out" a particular part of the series, such as specifically coloring bars, pie wedges, or clusters because they are an exception, represent future dates or specific dimension values, etc.

Quick Reference Instructions

This section contains instructions for the following topics:

- How to move the legend above the chart data
- How to change chart settings to always display all data labels

I. How to move the legend above the chart data

1. In the **Chart View**, open the **Additional Charting Options** dialog box
2. Go to the **Legends** tab
3. Select **Top** from the **Legends** drop-down list

II. How to change chart settings to always display all data labels

1. In the **Chart View**, open the **General Chart Properties** dialog box
2. Select **Always** from the **Show data labels** drop-down list

Bar Charts

Bar charts are one of the most widely used charts to compare groups of data against a common metric. Most users and designers are already very comfortable utilizing this type of chart. We've come up with a few best practices specific to bar charts which will come in handy when working within Oracle Business Intelligence to design powerful, professional-looking reports.

Best Practices

BP 3.5: *Bar charts should be two-dimensional and use the cylinder style.*

When creating a bar chart, you should always set the type to "2D" and the style to "cylinder". Although designers may be tempted to use 3D bar charts for presentation purposes, 2D charts are more easily interpreted than 3D charts with regards to their exact data representation. Using the cylinder style will give the charts a three-dimensional feel while allowing the user to more accurately examine the data. An example of a 2D vertical bar chart using the cylinder style is shown in Figure 3.5.

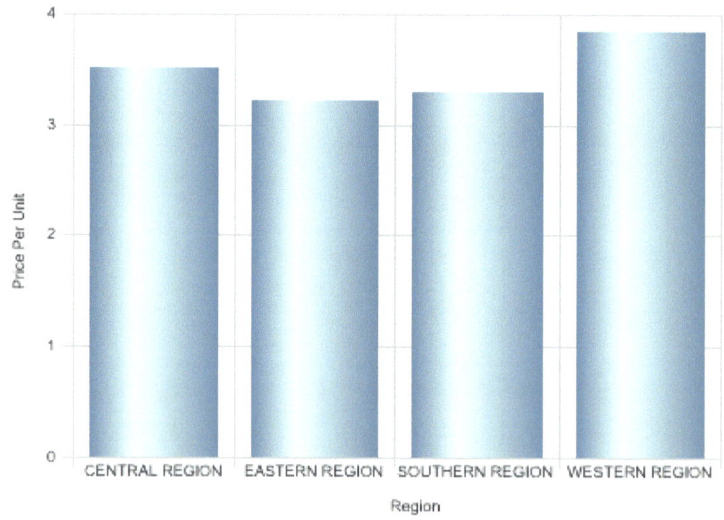

Figure 3.5 Two-dimensional vertical bar chart with cylinder-style bars.

***BP 3.6:** The right bar chart should be chosen for the space it will occupy, the number of items in the series, and the nature of the data being displayed. Vertical bar charts work well in wider spaces, with a fewer number of series values, and numeric data that is positive. Horizontal bar charts can accommodate more series values, fit in a narrower space in the dashboard, and reflect contrasts between positive and negative numbers more effectively.*

Most bar charts will be presented in a vertical style, as bar charts become difficult to read with too many bars on them. However, horizontal charts are an excellent alternative when chart characteristics demand them.

Quick Reference Instructions

This section contains instructions for the following topic:

I. How to create a bar chart using the two-dimensional cylinder style

1. In the **Results** tab, select the **Chart View**
2. Select **2D** from the **Type** drop-down list
3. Select **Cylinder** or **Default** from the **Style** drop-down list

Pie Charts

Another of the classic chart types is the pie chart. These charts are most often utilized when displaying groups of data in proportion to an entire data set. We've come up with a few tips to take into consideration when designing these commonly used charts within Oracle BI.

Best Practices

BP 3.7: *Pie charts should be designed using the 3-dimensional style, as these charts do not require reading data as it relates to an axis.*

In our opinion, this style is simply much more visually appealing than the familiar two-dimensional style. Since 3D pie charts do not present the same issue of being misinterpreted against axes as 3D bar charts, they should be used as opposed to 2D charts. The wedges are always shown in proper proportion; therefore the 3D look should not cause any problems with interpretation.

BP 3.8: *When a pie chart has many wedges, care should be taken to make sure the chart is legible, with consideration for using data and name label display on rollover (or always).*

Changing the option to display the value ***and*** name can be very helpful when so many wedges are displayed that the colors on the legend aren't differentiated well enough to easily determine their corresponding section in the chart. Changing the settings as described above would result in the chart shown in Figure 3.6.

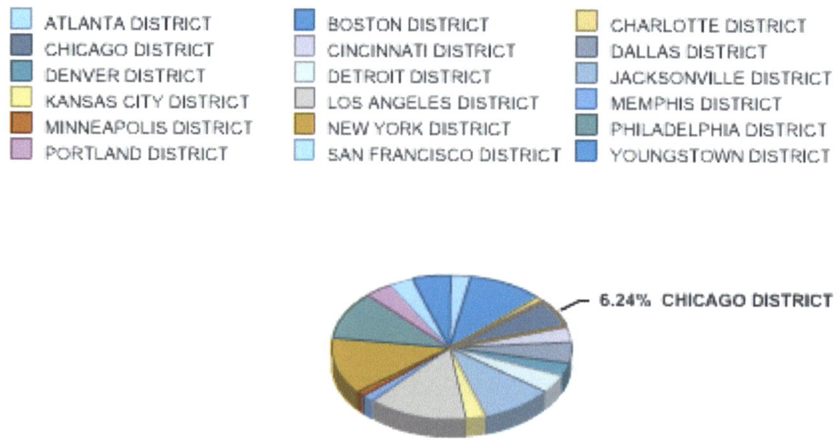

Figure 3.6 Pie chart with values and data labels set to display on rollover.

Quick Reference Instructions

This section contains instructions for the following topics:

- How to apply the three-dimensional style to a pie chart
- How to set the data labels within a pie chart to display both the data label and the value

I. How to apply the three-dimensional style to a pie chart

1. In the **Results** tab, select the **Chart View**
2. Select **3D** from the **Type** drop-down list

II. How to set the data labels within a pie chart to display both the data label and the value

1. In the **Results** tab, select the **Chart View**
2. Open the **Advanced properties** dialog box
3. Select **Name and Value** from the **Label Shows** drop-down list
4. Click **OK** to display the results

Line Bar Combination Charts

Line bar combo charts can be a great way to combine two separate metrics and study how they relate to each other as measured against a common attribute. These charts, when used effectively, can give insight into relationships between measures that the individual line and bar charts can't provide. The following are some common guidelines to consider when designing line bar combination charts.

Best Practices

BP 3.9: *Line bar combination work well when the metrics being measured in the line and the bar are dissimilar, but if they are similar, the left and right Y-axis should be forced to the same scale (available only in 10g version of OBIEE).*

When similar metrics are placed on the same combination chart and the left and right Y-axis are not forced to the same scale, the results can be confusing or misleading. For example, displaying sales dollars this year as the bar data and sales dollars last year as the line data may cause users to incorrectly assess the chart, because the two metrics on the y-axis (which are both dollars in this example) will be automatically scaled separately by the charting engine based on the two individual data sets – unless the checkbox in the Advanced properties is checked to force a common Y-axis scale. Designers may be tempted to manually reset the scale of the chart. This technique should be avoided, because when drilling or filtering on this data, the minimum and maximums on the y-axis will be retained in the new chart, which will skew the height of the bars and lines and make the chart difficult to read.

Figure 3.7 shows how the left and right Y-axis can assume different scales by using dollars in both the bar and line axis without forcing the same scale. The charting engine has automatically resized the right and left axis with different maximum numbers, causing the line data to appear higher than the bar data (making last year's sales look higher than this year's sales), when in fact they are much lower.

Another use of this type of chart would be to use unrelated metrics, such as an ordinal metric in the bar (like units or dollars) and a percentage or difference for the line (such as percent increase in price from last year). This can help display the relationship between the two metrics; if price was increased, did units or dollars increase as well?

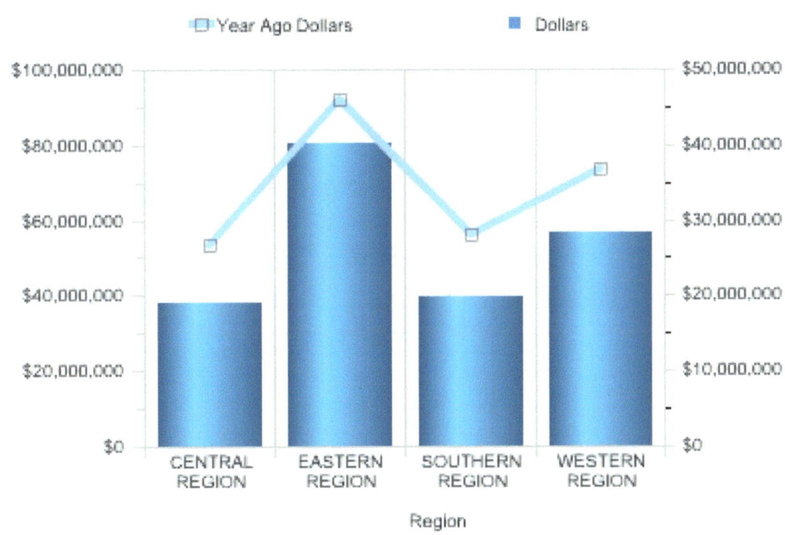

Figure 3.7 Incorrect use of a line bar combination chart. The line and bars are using the same metric with different scales on the y-axis.

Figure 3.8 shows an example of a better use of this chart, in that the bar axis displays dollars, and the line axis displays a percent change from the previous year. This use of the combination chart is much more meaningful because at a single glance, the user can immediately tell that both of the stronger regions also had stronger growth from the previous year.

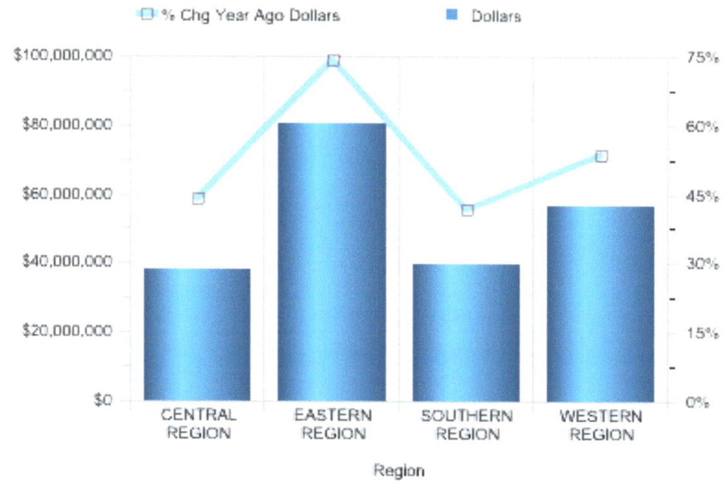

Figure 3.8 Correct use of a line bar combination chart. The line and bars are using separate metrics on the y-axis.

***BP 3.10:** When designing a line-bar combination chart, individual markers at each data point should replace a solid line if using a line could potentially imply a trend that does not exist or does not make sense.*

While line charts are frequently used either individually or in combination with a bar chart, they are often used incorrectly. When viewing a chart containing a line, many users will interpret a trend although the data points have no correlation in regards to the order they are presented. For example, Figure 3.9 below shows an example of a false trend against a non-time dimension.

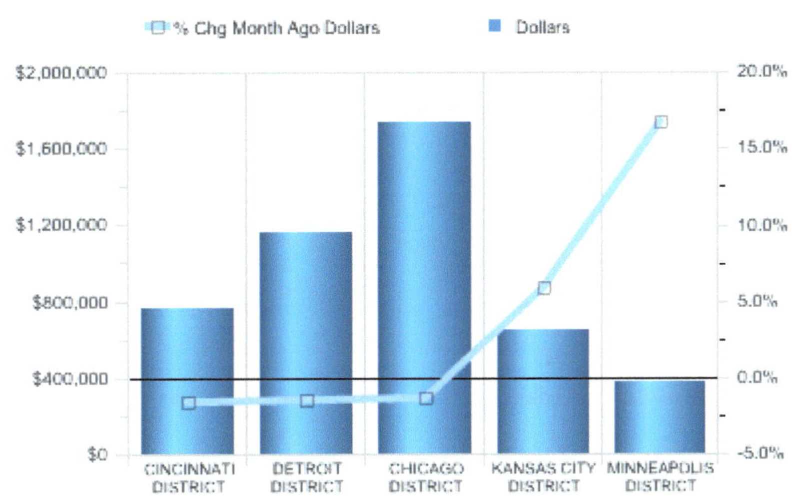

Figure 3.9 Line bar combination chart showing an example of a false trend against a non-time dimension.

A similar mistake can occur when the line chart improperly implies a real-time or "moment by moment" trend, when in fact the data may be aggregated no lower than a month or year. For example, in Figure 3.10, the chart shows a steady decline from year to year.

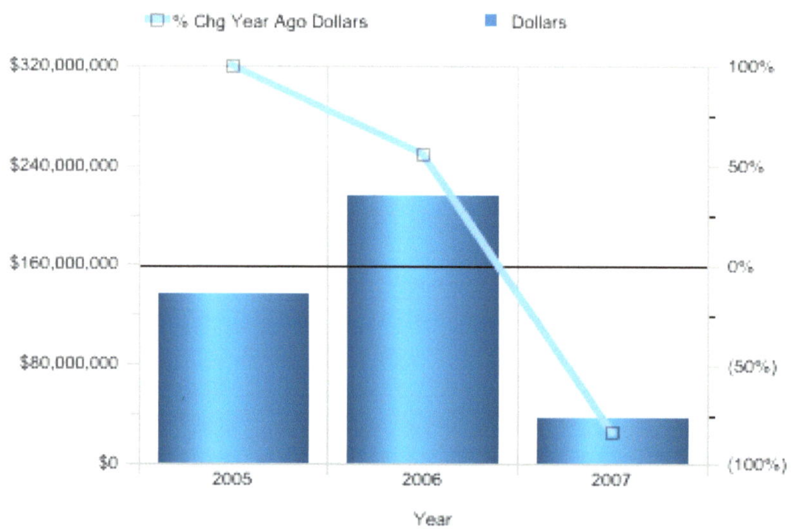

Figure 3.10 Line bar combination chart improperly implying a real-time trend.

The line in this case may lead the user to believe that the measure "% Year Ago Dollars" was on a consistent slide from one year to the next, when in fact, the measure may have climbed steadily for several months, then dropped significantly toward the end of the year, resulting in the negative percentage for the period as a whole. Keep in mind that even when trending across time, in most cases, the data is aggregated in "chunks" of time, and the trend line is only going to show the up or down difference from one "chunk" to the next. A better use of this chart type would be to drop the line and add point markers instead, such as in figure 3.11.

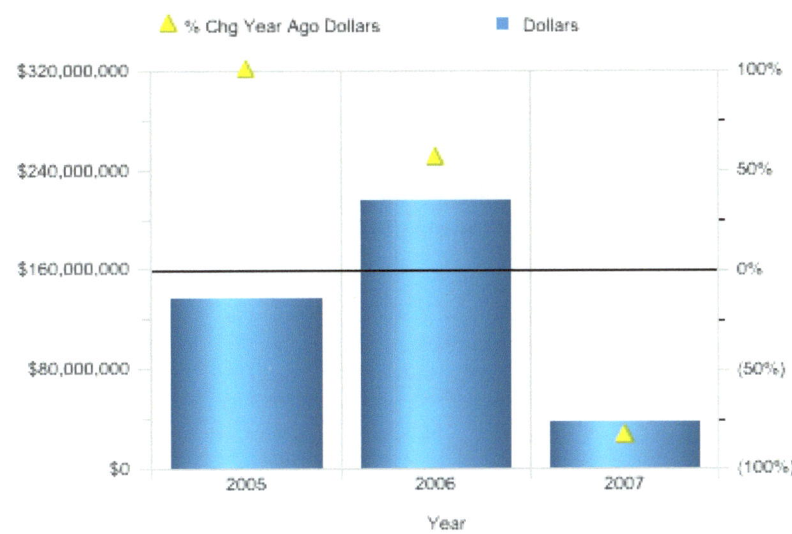

Figure 3.11 Line bar combination chart with lines removed and point markers added.

Quick Reference Instructions

This section contains instructions for the following topic:

I. Replacing a solid line with individual data markers within a line bar combination chart

1. In the **Chart View**, select **Line Bar Combo** from the **Graph** drop-down list
2. Check the boxes for the appropriate columns to display on each axis
3. Open the **Format Chart Data** dialog box
4. In the **Position** tab, uncheck the **Use Default** checkbox next to **Position 1**
5. Select **0** from the **Width** drop-down list in the **Line properties** area
6. Select **Triangle** from the **Type** drop-down list in the **Symbol** properties area
7. Click the **Color** box in the **Symbol** properties area
8. Select a color from the **Color Selector** window
9. Click **OK** to display the results

Bubble Charts

While the bubble chart may take some explanation to your end users, it uniquely allows simultaneous analysis of how three metrics interact. The bubble chart plots the three metrics on three axes: an x-axis, a y-axis, and a third "axis", which is shown as the size of the bubble. In Figure 3.12, we are plotting dollars, units and percent to plan. Ignoring for now the size of the bubble, you can see that the placement of the bubble relative to the x and y axes equates to the dollar and unit amount for each district shown in the tabular layout just below the bubble chart. The placement of the bubble provides a good deal of insight.

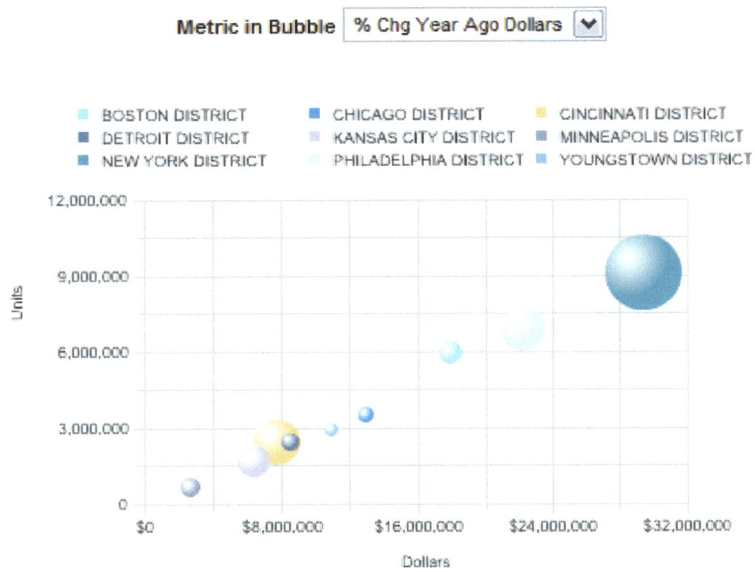

District	Units	Dollars	% Chg Year Ago Dollars
BOSTON DISTRICT	5,978,841	$17,964,053	41%
CHICAGO DISTRICT	3,540,658	$12,945,705	31%
CINCINNATI DISTRICT	2,410,117	$7,800,295	82%
DETROIT DISTRICT	2,452,047	$8,524,076	33%
KANSAS CITY DISTRICT	1,661,963	$6,432,032	57%
MINNEAPOLIS DISTRICT	704,254	$2,614,576	35%
NEW YORK DISTRICT	9,126,305	$29,328,594	134%
PHILADELPHIA DISTRICT	6,922,598	$22,206,245	81%
YOUNGSTOWN DISTRICT	2,915,809	$10,861,109	27%

Figure 3.12 Example of a bubble chart along with tabular data.

For example, we can immediately tell from the chart in Figure 3.12 that Boston, the third highest selling district, sells more units on average per dollar than the other districts. We can determine this because the Boston "bubble" is slightly above the straight line formed from the worst to the best district. That fact might tell a VP of Sales that the Boston district is discounting more than other districts; or selling lower priced items than other districts; etc. Where the bubble chart becomes powerful though, is in also looking at that third metric, indicated by the size of the bubble. In this case, we've plotted the percent change in sales dollars from last year in the bubble, and immediately, we can tell that the best performing district by dollars and units (New York) also had the highest percent change in sales from last year.

Best Practices

BP 3.11: *Within a bubble chart, the metrics plotted on the x and y-axes should be metrics that will have a good spread between elements that are being displayed.*

For example, if all of the districts in Figure x had a quota of $40 million, it wouldn't make sense to plot "Quota" on the x or y, because the bubbles would all be stacked in a single row, or worse, they would overlay each other. It is better to plot more contrasting metrics on these axes.

BP 3.12: *Data plotted in the bubble within bubble charts should be based on a metric that has a relatively narrow spread.*

This is because the size of the bubble is generated based on a relative comparison of all of the elements in the chart; so for example, trying to plot dollars in the bubble would not work well if one district had a dollar amount dozens or hundreds of times larger than the next district. The size of the bubble for the single district would overwhelm the size of all other bubbles. Good examples of measures with a narrower spread are percent changes, percent to totals, and averages. These measures make perfect candidates for bubble data.

BP 3.13: *The white space on a bubble chart should be removed by using the "Zoom to Data Range" option.*

Often, when a bubble chart is first generated, a vast majority of the space on the chart will not be used. A bubble chart can also become hard to read when several of the bubbles become crowded in one portion of the chart. Using the "Zoom to Data Range" option will automatically adjust the axes to remove as much unused space as possible while keeping all plotted data within the viewing range.

BP 3.14: *When designing a bubble chart, a column selector should be used to allow the user to flip between several different metrics to be plotted within the bubble.*

Use a column selector as in our example in Figure 3.13 to allow the user to flip between several different metrics to be plotted in the bubble. In this example, we're allowing the user to flip from "% Change Year Ago Units" to several of the percent change metrics. This would allow the user to see how the strong and weak regions are doing in terms of growth, all at a glance.

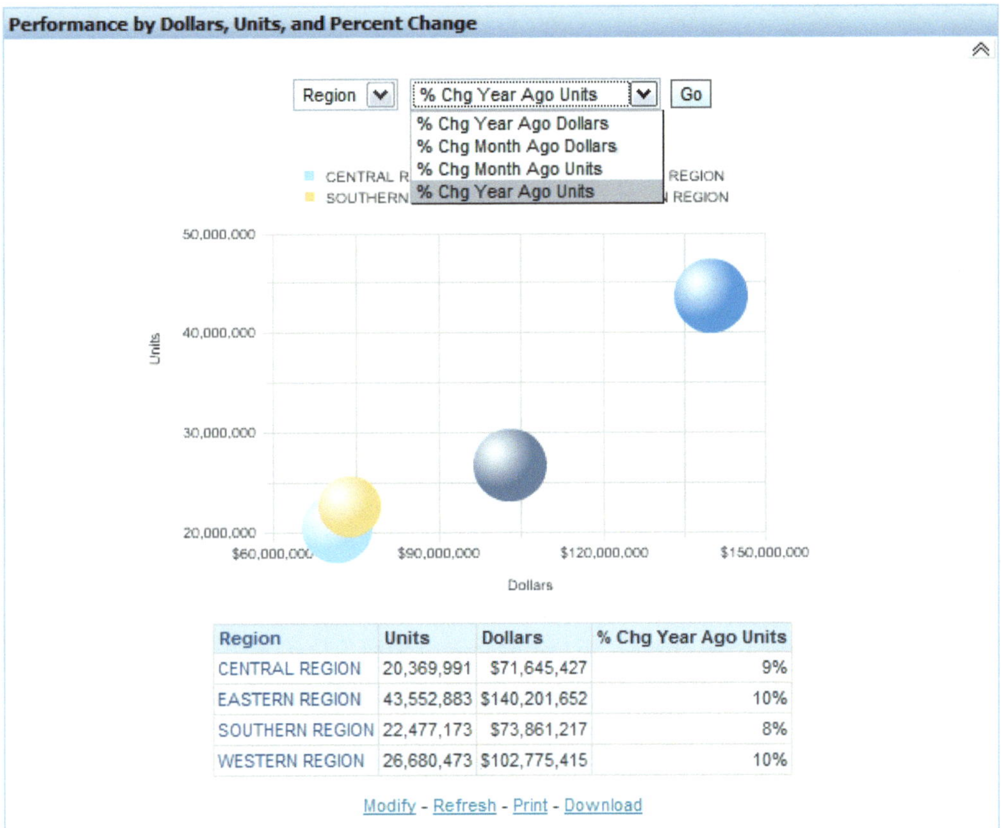

Region	Units	Dollars	% Chg Year Ago Units
CENTRAL REGION	20,369,991	$71,645,427	9%
EASTERN REGION	43,552,883	$140,201,652	10%
SOUTHERN REGION	22,477,173	$73,861,217	8%
WESTERN REGION	26,680,473	$102,775,415	10%

Figure 3.13 Bubble chart report using column selectors.

BP 3.15: A tabular view should be placed in the compound layout beneath a bubble chart.

We mentioned in the general section that when any type of chart becomes too cluttered, the designer might need to add a table to the report. The tabular view can be used for reference if the bubble sizes are close or overlaid. This technique can also be very valuable when a larger number of elements are plotted because the colors in the legend may be similar and difficult to distinguish.

Quick Reference Instructions

This section contains instructions for the following topic:

I. How to remove the white space on a bubble chart by using the "Zoom to Data Range" option

1. In the **Chart View**, open the **Axis Scaling** dialog box
2. From the **Left** tab, select the **Zoom to Data Range** radio button option under **Axis Limits**
3. Repeat **Step 2** from the **Bottom** tab
4. Click **OK** to view the results

Scatter Charts

The intent of a scatter chart is to imply insight into "clusters" of data that might paint an important picture about the business. A scatter chart uses two metrics, one on the y-axis and one on the x-axis, and data points are displayed across the grid. In this type of chart, it isn't necessary to display the label of each data point – that information could be retrieved using report navigation to a detailed report on each data point. More important is uncovering how and where clusters appear on the chart.

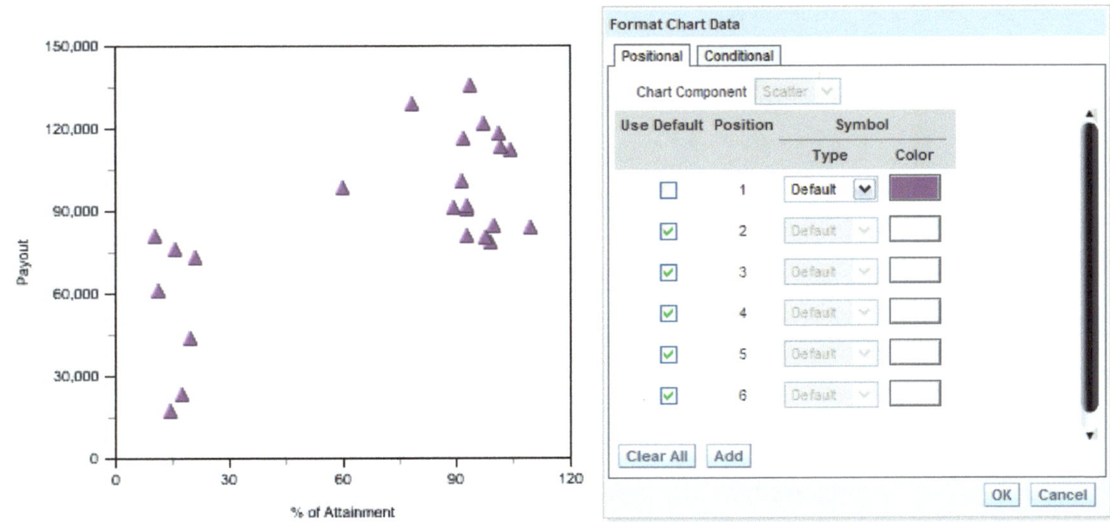

Figure 3.14 Scatter chart and settings

In Figure 3.14, two metrics are being compared for correlation, namely a payout of commission in dollars, and a percent of attainment in regards to a quota. Two clusters are immediately apparent, showing that entities (which could be sales representatives, districts, regions, etc.) that achieve 90 - 120% of their quota, are earning the highest commissions, ranging from about $75,000 to $130,000.

What's more interesting here is that there is a major gap between the two clusters, implying that there are very few "middle of the road" quota achievers -they are either very good or very poor. The second interesting observation is that the cluster on the lower left is elongated, which shows that entities with a very low level of quota attainment are earning as much as the lower level of the highest quota achievers. This might imply to a VP of Sales that he needs to reduce the commission rate until a higher level of the quota has been hit. As you can see, scatter charts can provide unique insight that can't easily be obtained through the use of other charts or tables.

Chapter 4: Other Views and Objects

There are many view types within Oracle BI that can be used to enhance the main view types we have already covered such as tables and charts. In this section, we cover three of them and provide some tips to assist you in getting the most out of them. We start with view selectors, which are a very simple yet powerful way to both conserve dashboard real estate and provide users with many options within dashboards. Next we touch on column selectors, which are another way users can gain access to many different variations on the same report with just a few clicks of the mouse. Finally, we discuss the filters view, which plays an important role in any report by verifying that the user knows exactly what subset of data is being analyzed.

View Selectors

The use of view selectors allows the user to choose what type of report view will best provide insight about the information they are to examine. View selectors simply provide a drop down list at the top of the report that gives the user the option to choose between any number of tables and charts pertaining to the report data. This view type is a great way to combine multiple related views in the same report, and as you'll read below, should be used liberally when designing user-friendly dashboards.

Best Practices

BP 4.1: View selectors should be used whenever possible to maximize dashboard space.

In general, reports with a view selector should contain at least two different types of charts and one grid view (table, pivot table). This allows a user to analyze information from multiple perspectives and choose which one is their favorite. Including a table or pivot table allows the user to switch to the actual data rather than a graphical view, for those cases where a chart may simply have too many data points to make sense (such as a pie chart with dozens of wedges, or a bar chart with dozens of columns).

BP 4.2: The words "Select a View" should be used for the dialog to the left of a view selector.

Using this wordage will ensure the user is not confused as to what exactly he or she is selecting. One exception is when the view selector is used to mimic pivoting of facts from rows to columns (by creating two or more pivot table views within a single report). In that case, the standard is to have the words "Metric Location:" to the left of the view selector.

BP 4.3: Chart and table names within a view selector should be given meaningful names so the user can easily determine what type of view and what data will be displayed.

Each view option should have a descriptive name such as the view type and metric(s) displayed, such as "Pie Chart of Sales Dollars" or "Bar Chart Comparing Forecasted and Actual Sales Dollars". Tabular views should usually be named "Detailed Data" or "Tabular Data". See Figure 4.1 for further examples of properly named views.

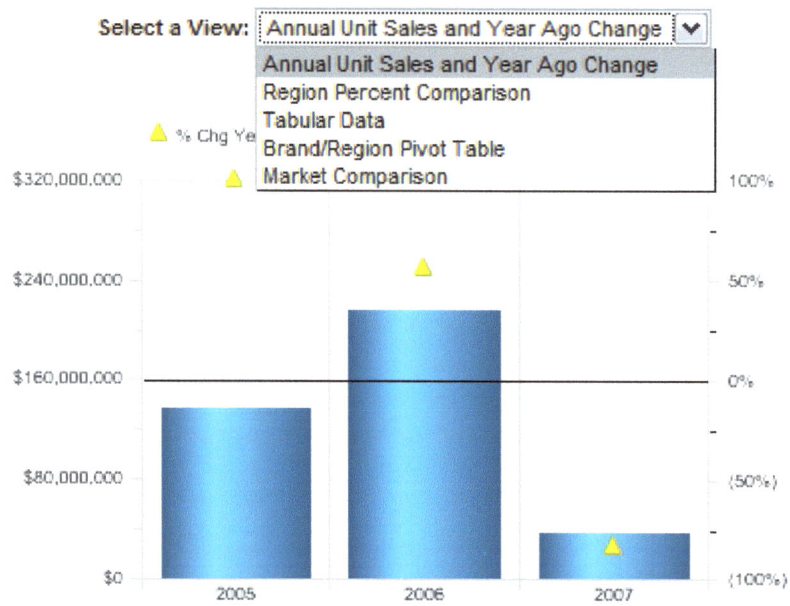

Figure 4.1 View selector displaying many properly named views.

BP 4.4: *When a chart is drillable, the user should be provided with a view selector to allow switching between the charted view and a numeric view.*

It was briefly mentioned in the general charting section that drill-down reports should be taken into account when deciding whether to display data labels. Here's another good example of when the ability to drill should be considered during report design. The practice of adding a grid view is to allow the user to switch to this view of data in the event that their drill-down has caused a chart display to become less legible. For example, if the user drilled into a bar on a bar chart, and the chart returned with dozens of bars at the lower level of hierarchy, as demonstrated in Figure 4.2. The user could switch to the grid view to have a legible view of the data, and could switch back to the chart view if subsequent levels of drill down have a more manageable number of elements returned. The standard is to provide the grid view in a format that is approximately as wide as the original chart view to maintain spacing on the dashboard.

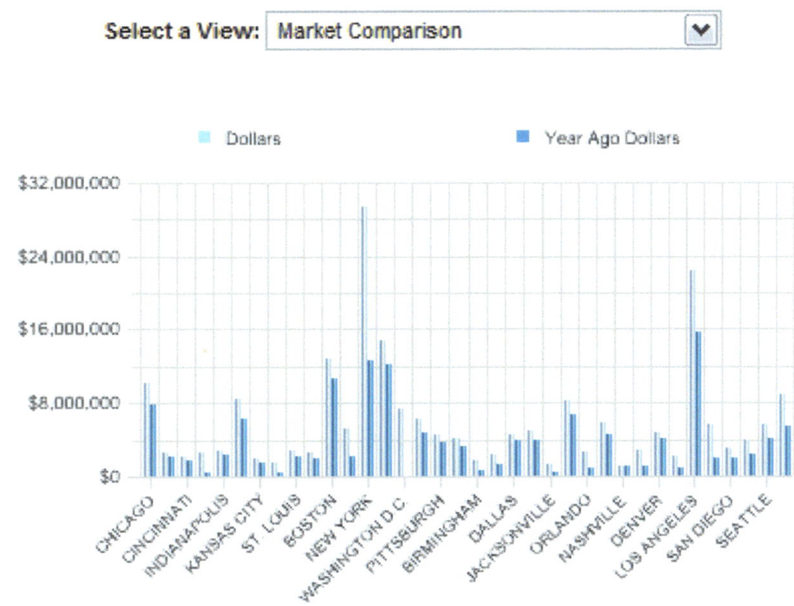

Figure 4.2 Example of a crowded bar chart. A tabular view should be offered in the view selector as this chart data may be difficult for some to read.

By making a tabular or pivot table version of the report available through the view selector, as in Figure 4.3, the user can continue to analyze the data in an easily understandable format. The user could even subsequently drill on a year or market, and then switch back to a charted view if the number of data points lent themselves to a charted display.

Select a View: Market / Sales Pivot Table

Market		2005	2006	2007
CHICAGO	Units	2,285,340	2,806,320	534,184
	Dollars	$7,739,753	$10,301,643	$2,040,639
	Year Ago Dollars		$7,739,753	$10,301,643
	% Chg Year Ago Dollars	100%	33%	(80%)
MILWAUKEE	Units	613,716	734,338	77,635
	Dollars	$2,154,122	$2,644,062	$322,966
	Year Ago Dollars		$2,154,122	$2,644,062
	% Chg Year Ago Dollars	100%	23%	(88%)
CINCINNATI	Units	474,235	634,972	98,267
	Dollars	$1,633,938	$2,209,883	$388,194
	Year Ago Dollars		$1,633,938	$2,209,883
	% Chg Year Ago Dollars	100%	35%	(82%)
COLUMBUS	Units	116,937	794,856	121,919
	Dollars	$352,618	$2,675,217	$500,442
	Year Ago Dollars		$352,618	$2,675,217
	% Chg Year Ago Dollars	100%	659%	(81%)
INDIANAPOLIS	Units	777,771	980,289	160,584
	Dollars	$2,304,908	$2,915,195	$490,759
	Year Ago Dollars		$2,304,908	$2,915,195
	% Chg Year Ago Dollars	100%	26%	(83%)

Figure 4.3 Pivot chart showing the same data from Figure 4.2 as well as additional metrics.

Quick Reference Instructions

This section contains instructions for the following topics:

- How to edit the text used for the dialog to the left of a view selector
- How to edit the names of the individual views within a view selector

I. How to edit the text used for the dialog to the left of a view selector

1. From the **Results** tab, select the **View Selector** layout view
2. Enter “Select a View” or other text in the **Caption** text box

II. <u>How to edit the names of the individual views within a view selector</u>

1. From the **Results** tab, select the **View Selector** layout view
2. Add the appropriate views to the **Views Included** area by highlighting them in the **Available Views** area and clicking the **right arrow**
3. Highlight a view and click the **Rename** button
4. Enter the appropriate name and click **OK** to return to the View Selector layout view.

Column Selectors

Column selectors allow users to manipulate a report by replacing columns with other columns, generating a completely different view of a report. It could be replacing one metric with another, a parent level hierarchy column with a child, or one dimensional attribute with another. This is a design strategy that can help avoid a report that is 15 columns wide. This technique also avoids repetitive user requests to build slight variations of existing reports. Using column selectors, they can make the variation themselves. As shown in Figure 4.4, designers can even include cross-dimensional attributes, which in this case allow the user to turn a region summary report into a district, brand, or color report.

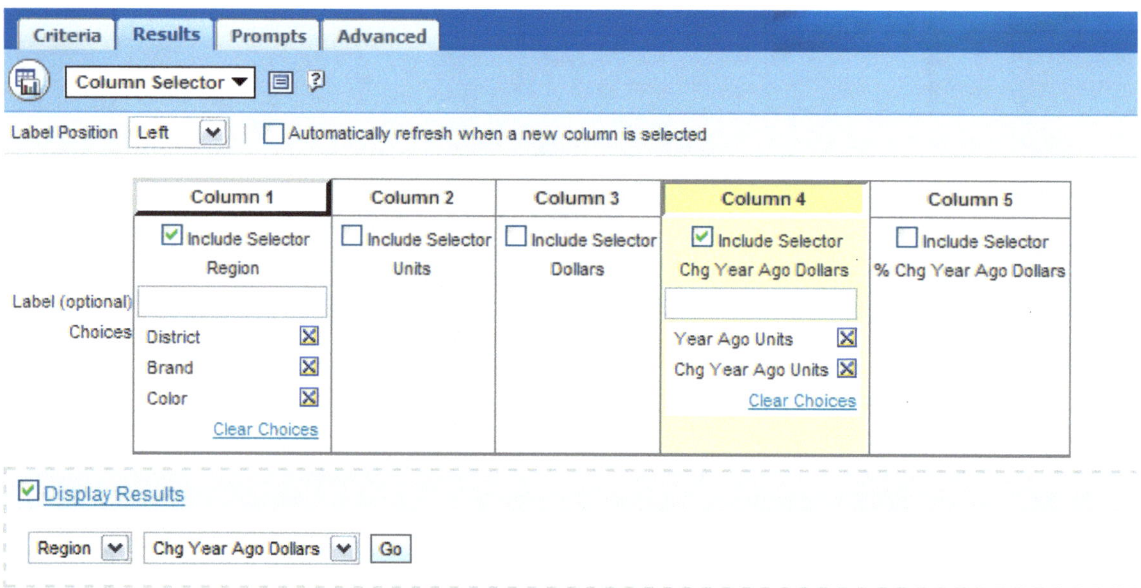

Figure 4.4 Column Selector View in Answers.

The settings in Figure 4.4 will result in the column selector shown in Figure 4.5, which gives the user eleven permutations beyond the original report layout.

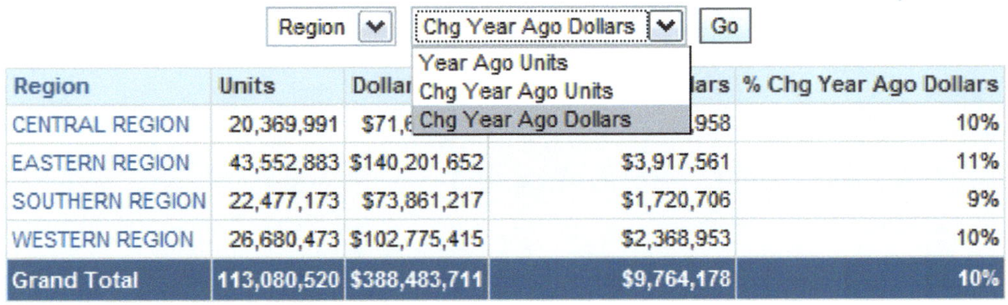

Region	Units	Dollar	lars	% Chg Year Ago Dollars
CENTRAL REGION	20,369,991	$71,(	958	10%
EASTERN REGION	43,552,883	$140,201,652	$3,917,561	11%
SOUTHERN REGION	22,477,173	$73,861,217	$1,720,706	9%
WESTERN REGION	26,680,473	$102,775,415	$2,368,953	10%
Grand Total	113,080,520	$388,483,711	$9,764,178	10%

Figure 4.5 Report containing two column selectors.

Best Practices

BP 4.5: *When a single column selector is used, the "Go" button should be turned off. When more than one column selector is used, the "Go" button should be enabled so that the user can make all of their selections before refreshing the report.*

Notice in Figure 4.6 that the "Automatically refresh when a new column is selected" option is unchecked, which causes the "Go" button to appear next to the column selectors. By default, this option will be checked and the "Go" button will not appear. When multiple columns within a view are available for change, enabling the "Go" button will allow users to make all of the intended changes without causing the report to automatically refresh after each selection. This can help prevent executing wasteful queries against your database.

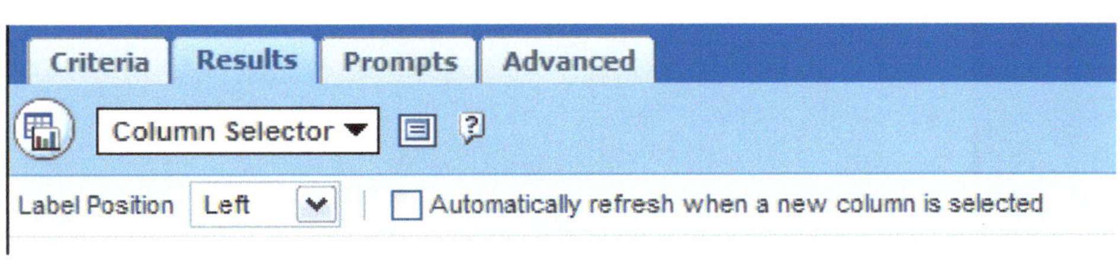

Figure 4.6 "Go" button checkbox.

Filters View

The filters view is one of the objects that can be added to the compound layout of a report. The filters view explains the entire filter criteria used in the report. Figure 4.7 demonstrates how to add a filters view.

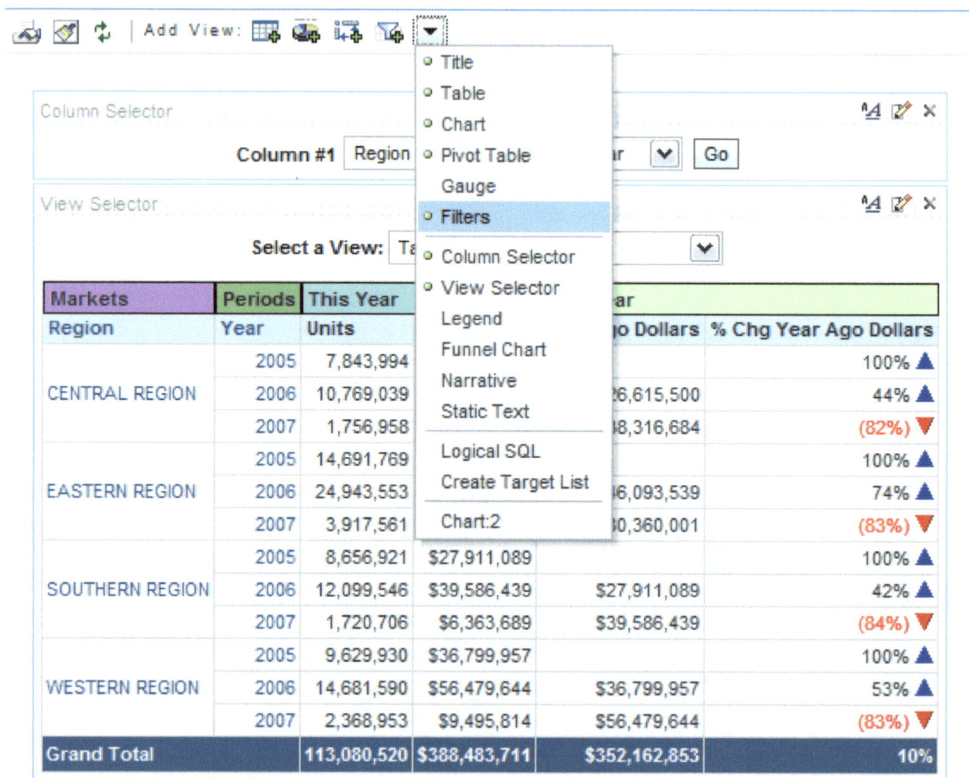

Figure 4.7 Filters view option within the add view drop-down list.

The filters view will be added to the bottom of the Compound Layout.

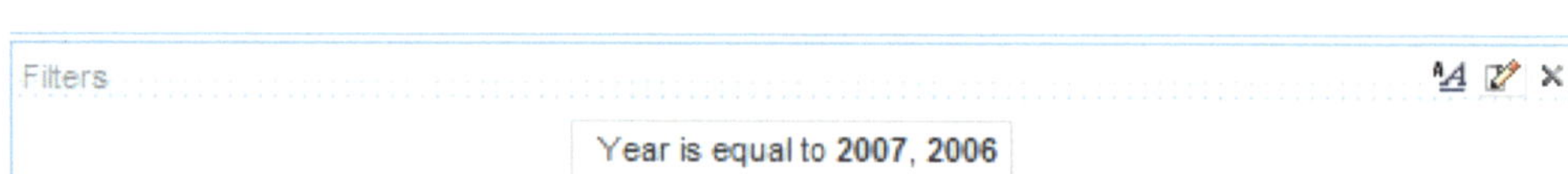

Figure 4.8 Filters view showing that only data from the years 2006 and 2007 is currently displayed.

Best Practices

BP 4.6: *Reports that utilize filters should also include a filters view at the bottom of the report, unless the filter criteria are obvious to all users based on the contents of the report.*

Adding a filter object to a report is especially helpful if the filter criteria are not obvious from the content of the report. For example, if a dashboard prompt allows the user to filter on data elements that are not displayed within the rows or columns of a tabular view, pivot table, or chart, the addition of the filter object is required, especially if the report is going to be printed.

In the example report below, the prompt at the top of the dashboard page has allowed the user to filter on year, but year does not appear anywhere in the chart. Therefore, the filter object is necessary to show the year that this information is based on. On the other hand if it is obvious from the report content what is being filtered, then the filter object is not required. For example, if a report is filtered on three regions and the three regions are displayed in a table, pivot table or chart, then the filter object may not be needed.

BP 4.7*: A background and border can be added to the filters view to make it stand out from the rest of the report.*

By default, a filters view will have no border or background color, so it can easily become lost in the content of the report. We recommend formatting the filters view with a gray background and black border to help set it off from the rest of the report. The idea is to make the filter block apparent, but not flashy or obtrusive. Some find the solid grey box to be aesthetically displeasing, though, so other styles can be attempted. Figure 4.9 demonstrates the new appearance of the filters view using the recommended format.

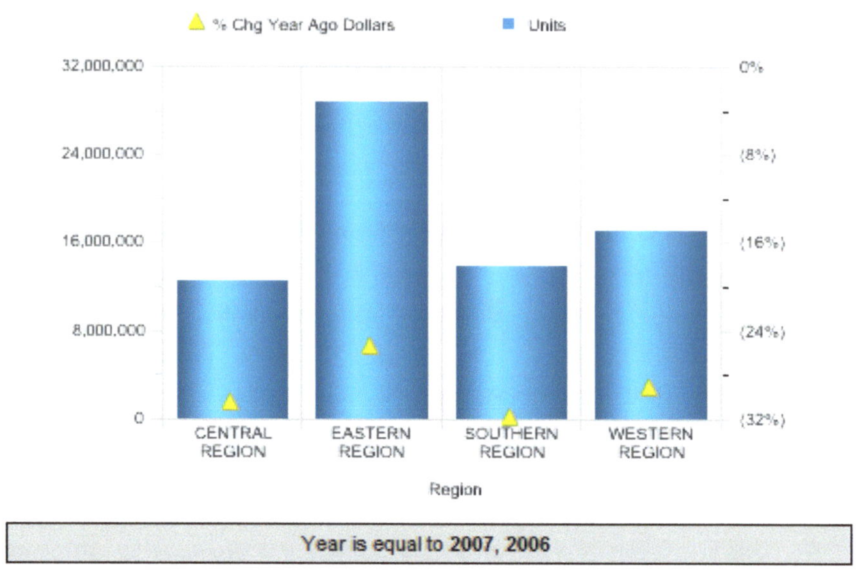

Figure 4.9 Example of a report with a properly formatted filters view.

Quick Reference Instructions

This section contains instructions for the following topics:

- How to add a filters view to the report
- How to format a filters view

I. How to add a Filters View to the report

1. In the **Results** tab, click the **Add View** link
2. Select **Filters**
3. A **Filters View** will be added to the bottom of the **Compound Layout**

II. How to format a Filters View

1. In the **Results** tab, select **Compound Layout** in the **View** drop-down menu
2. Click the **Format View** button located in the **Filters View**
3. In the **Edit Format** dialog box, select the desired format settings
4. Click **OK**

Chapter 5: Reports

In Oracle BI, the term "Request" is synonymous with what many people would call a "Report". In this text, we use the two terms interchangeably. In Oracle BI, reports are built in Answers, and are then typically assembled together alongside other reports to create a dashboard. A report usually contains many different views and renderings of the same data columns. These views are organized together using the compound layout view. The compound layout can be used to display many different views and objects, such as:

- Grid views (tables and pivot tables)
- Chart views (bubble charts, bar charts, etc.)
- Explanatory views (filters, legends, etc.)
- Functional objects (column selectors and view selectors)

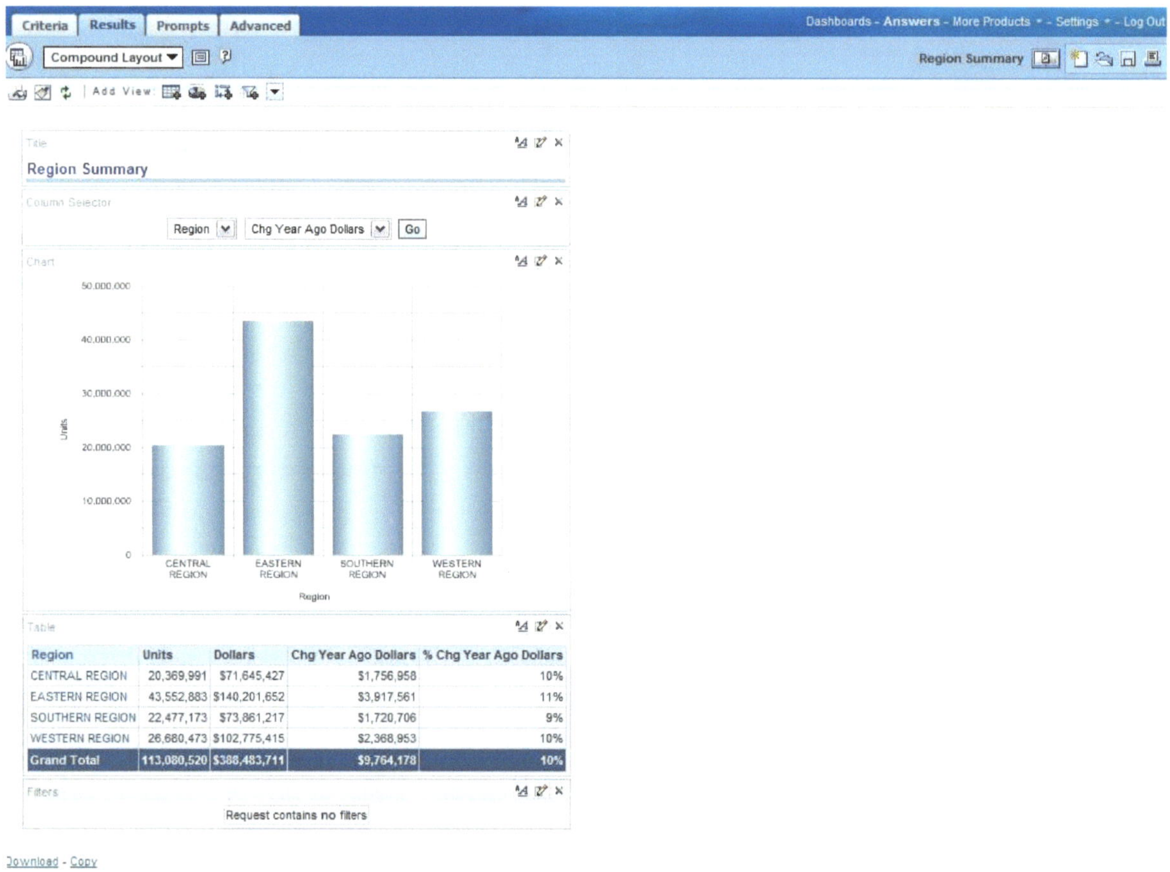

Figure 5.1 Compound Layout View showing title, column selector, chart, table, and filters views.

Figure 5.1 shows the compound layout view for a request with several different views included. While each of these views and objects has their own respective sections in this guide, as a whole they come together to form a report. And as such, while each of these topics has its own individual best practices, the report as a whole has its own best practices, each of which may relate to one or more of these individual topics.

In this chapter, we reiterate some of the best practices of the individual report components in addition to introducing those best practices that apply to the report as a whole. We will also present a few additional features and functionalities that may be useful when building a report.

Reporting Basics

Two of the most important factors to consider when designing a report are readability and usability. Below, we will briefly review three of the best methods to enhance these two factors. The methods are:

- Breaking up large tables into smaller chunks
- Using column selectors
- Using view selectors

Breaking up Reports

Large tables should be broken into multiple pivot tables in order to make the width fit into a single screen. For example, if a report requires 15 columns, and that causes the report width to be too wide, the report can be broken into three, five column wide pivot table views within the same report. To the user, this will appear as a nicely stacked pivot table report with three layers of metrics.

This can be done by selecting all 15 metrics within the criteria tab, adding three pivot table views, and then including five metrics and excluding ten metrics within each pivot table view. This style of report will still allow the user to export all 15 metrics into Excel (since all 15 metrics are included in the report) and view all 15 metrics on a single screen. The difference is they shouldn't have to scroll from left to right, which is cumbersome with most mice. Instead, they can scroll up and down, which is typically easier.

View Selectors

An alternative is to place the multiple pivot tables into a view selector, showing one pivot table at a time. View selectors should also be used to reduce the number of charts displayed at once.

Column Selectors

When all metrics are not required to be displayed simultaneously, column selectors should be used to allow the user to select the columns that they wish to have displayed simultaneously, while limiting the total number of columns so there is no horizontal scrolling required.

Best Practices

Before we introduce the best practices that apply to reports as a whole, let's review some best practices that have already been stated in previous chapters:

> ***BP 2.10:*** *If a report has a pivot table with drillable elements, then the report should make the pivot table available through a view selector that also contains a tabular view.*
>
> ***BP 3.3****: When a report containing a chart is likely to be printed, and data labels are displayed on rollover, a tabular or pivot table view should be made available by placing it beneath the chart view within the report.*
>
> ***BP 4.1:*** *View selectors should be used whenever possible to maximize dashboard space.*
>
> ***BP 4.6:*** *Reports that utilize filters should also include a filters view at the bottom of the report, unless the filter criteria are obvious to all users based on the contents of the report.*

The remainder of this section discusses best practices that apply to reports as a whole.

BP 5.1: *Reports and dashboards should be designed to fit on the lowest expected screen resolution of its users. 800 x 600 screen resolution has traditionally been used as the lower limit, but today 1024 x 768 resolutions are more common.*

> Since reports are almost always placed into dashboards, they must be designed to appropriately fit into the column in which they will be added. Check with your IT department on the lowest resolution that you would expect to find on computer screens and laptops.
>
> A good practice to ensure that reports are not too wide is to set the designer's screen resolution to the resolution recommend by the IT department, which will ensure that all reports and dashboards will fit their allocated spaces.

BP 5.2: *If a report is too large to fit in a dashboard and cannot be broken down into smaller chunks, then the report should not be displayed in a dashboard. Instead, it can be made available through Answers, through the folder section on a dashboard, or as a navigate-to-detail report.*

As mentioned previously, there are a few different ways to reduce the size of a report; however, reducing the size may not be an option for some reports. For example, the following reports cannot be reduced in size:

- A report that has been designed for printing
- A report where the design is based on regulatory requirements

In these cases, the best option may be to make the report available through outside of the Dashboard.

Quick Reference Instructions

This section contains instructions for the following topics:

I. How to save a report as a PDF file

1. In the **Results** tab, select **Compound Layout** in the **View** drop-down menu
2. Click on the **Print this analysis** button on the far right of the screen (button looks like a printer with a piece of paper coming out)
3. In the **Print this analysis** pop-up menu, select **PDF**
4. A new window will appear containing the PDF version of the report; click the **Save** button in the new window to save the PDF to the desired location

Ranking Reports

One type of report which many managers and executives find valuable is a ranking report. It's vital to any organization to know how its different groups are performing in comparison with each other. Data comparing measures for separate divisions or geographical areas is most often found in pie or bar charts, which can be very helpful, but in order for the users to get a quick glance at how everyone stacks up, a ranking report should also be included somewhere in the dashboard. This can be accomplished either by placing a table directly in a request which already includes a chart, or by creating a new report all together. Whichever method is selected, we'd like to share a few tips on additional steps that can be done when creating ranking reports and how those extra steps can result in a more flexible report after being placed on a dashboard.

Best Practices

***BP 5.3**: A ranking column should be added to a tabular view when creating a ranking report.*

Often when creating tabular reports comparing people or groups, designers will simply sort by a specific metric instead of including a new column. This can be a quick way to show who is near the top or bottom, but this will not help to determine specific ranks in a large report returning many rows. For instance, when examining Figure 5.2, a manager may want to know that Nashville is ranked 16th in percent change in dollars from last year, as opposed to "somewhere near the middle of the pack".

Market	Dollars	Chg Year Ago Dollars	% Chg Year Ago Dollars ▼
WASHINGTON D.C.	$8,912,749	$388,389	20% ▲
COLUMBUS	$3,528,277	$121,919	17% ▲
OKLAHOMA CITY/TULSA	$2,389,214	$76,380	14% ▲
HARTFORD/NEW HAVEN	$8,177,640	$301,463	13% ▲
SAN DIEGO	$5,621,012	$168,607	12% ▲
NEW ORLEANS/MOBILE	$4,424,457	$113,272	12% ▲
SALT LAKE CITY/BOISE	$3,369,534	$76,311	11% ▼
ST. LOUIS	$5,593,864	$133,762	11% ▼
ORLANDO	$3,900,782	$122,370	11% ▼
CHICAGO	$20,082,035	$534,184	11% ▼
BIRMINGHAM	$2,625,099	$66,727	11% ▼
DENVER	$10,070,137	$241,681	11% ▼
LOS ANGELES	$42,230,060	$1,124,897	11% ▼
NEW YORK	$46,497,637	$1,286,485	11% ▼
JACKSONVILLE	$1,944,671	$59,246	10% ▼
NASHVILLE	$2,410,374	$55,856	10% ▼
CLEVELAND	$12,429,258	$281,306	10% ▼
PHILADELPHIA	$29,827,430	$822,764	10% ▼
CINCINNATI	$4,232,015	$98,267	10% ▼
DETROIT	$16,404,481	$410,685	10% ▼
DALLAS	$9,370,939	$205,726	10% ▼
TAMPA	$11,292,240	$319,046	10% ▼
HOUSTON	$9,789,715	$209,[illegible]	9% ▼
PITTSBURGH	$8,884,470	$182,[illegible]	9% ▼
RALEIGH/DURHAM	$4,057,621	$101,280	9% ▼
PORTLAND	$6,854,027	$126,517	9% ▼
INDIANAPOLIS	$5,710,862	$160,584	9% ▼
ATLANTA	$7,943,643	$142,506	9% ▼

Figure 5.2 Ranking report without a ranking column.

In Figure 5.3, we have created a ranking report that displays the top ten markets ranked by percent change in sales compared with last year. There is another reason why the ranking column should be added to any ranking report that we will explain in the best practice below.

Rank	Market	Dollars	Year Ago Dollars	% Chg Year Ago Dollars
1	WASHINGTON D.C.	$8,912,749	$7,416,173	20% ▲
2	COLUMBUS	$3,528,277	$3,027,835	17% ▲
3	OKLAHOMA CITY/TULSA	$2,389,214	$2,103,782	14% ▲
4	HARTFORD/NEW HAVEN	$8,177,640	$7,262,962	13% ▲
5	SAN DIEGO	$5,621,012	$5,016,404	12% ▲
6	NEW ORLEANS/MOBILE	$4,424,457	$3,949,671	12% ▲
7	SALT LAKE CITY/BOISE	$3,369,534	$3,022,901	11% ▲
8	ST. LOUIS	$5,593,864	$5,023,396	11% ▲
9	ORLANDO	$3,900,782	$3,503,515	11% ▲
10	CHICAGO	$20,082,035	$18,041,396	11% ▲

Records 1 - 10

Figure 5.3 Ranking Report containing a ranking column and set to display ten records at a time.

***BP 5.4**: When creating a top or bottom "n" report, change the number of rows displayed instead of using filters to sort out top or bottom data.*

When creating top or bottom "n" reports, instead of filtering on the ranking column (for example, filtering on a ranking column where "Rank is Less Than or Equal to 10" or using the filter operator to get the "Top or Bottom n", we suggest that you not apply any filtering at all, and instead reset the number of rows displayed in a tabular layout to the number you would like to show as top or bottom. For example, we've set the number of rows displayed to ten in Figure 5.3. This allows the user to use the same report to immediately get top or bottom results, simply by sorting on any metric column. It also allows them to see the next ten, and the next ten, etc., something they would not get if you had filtered off everything else. This is another good reason to display the ranking column within your report. If the users are allowed to navigate to the next ten results or straight to the bottom ten results, they can use this column to easily determine the rankings of the rows currently displayed. Combining this approach with the ability to re-sort the report on the dashboard allows you perform top and bottom rankings quickly in the same report.

Quick Reference Instructions

This section contains instructions for the following topics:

- How to add a ranking column to a tabular report
- How to create a top or bottom "n" report without using filters

I. How to add a ranking column to a tabular report

1. From the **Results** tab, select the **Table View**
2. Add a duplicate of the column by which you will be ranking the rows by clicking on the column in the **Selection Pane** to the left
3. Open the **Edit Column Formula** dialog box
4. Click the **Function...** button to open the **Insert Function** dialog box
5. Select **Rank** from the list of functions within the **Aggregate** group
6. Click **OK** and the column name should now appear within the parentheses of the **Rank** function.
7. Click **OK** again to view the results
8. Click the **Order By** button in the **Rank** column to sort by rank
9. Change the column heading and reposition the column as desired

II. How to create a top or bottom "n" report without using filters

1. From the **Results** tab, select the **Table View**
2. Open the **Edit View** dialog box by clicking the **Table View Properties** icon
3. Enter the desired number of rows to be displayed in the **Rows per Page** text box
4. Click the **Enable column sorting in Dashboards** checkbox

Custom HTML Reports

As a web-based product, Oracle BI allows custom HTML to be placed into reports as part of the "Calculation" definition of any metric. Figure 5.4 uses custom HTML to overlay two metrics -- actual inventory versus inventory goal. The downside is that the PDF converter does not properly convert HTML code, so you will have to turn off the print to PDF option for these reports.

Figure 5.4 Report using custom HTML.

Figure 5.5 shows the HTML code that was used to create the report in Figure 5.4. The formula in this code uses a combination of CASE logic to allow an indicator to be color coded based on severity, and HTML programming to overlay two metrics, while fitting the size of the "bars" to fit within the given space. This formula was added via the "Calculation" tab within the "Indicator" column.

Figure 5.5 HTML formula used to create the report in Figure 5.4

```
CASE

WHEN (Measures.”Instock”) / Measures.”Instock Goal” < .5 THEN

    '<table><tr><td style="padding-left:0" width=' || CAST(Measures.”Instock Goal” AS
    VARCHAR(20)) || ' bgcolor=#7F00FF height=16> <table><tr><td width=' ||
    CAST(Measures.”Instock” AS VARCHAR(20)) || ' bgcolor=#FF6666 height=12>
    </td></tr></table> </td><td class=oc>' || CAST(Measures.”Instock Goal” AS
    VARCHAR(20)) || '</td></tr></table>'

WHEN (Measures.”Instock”) / Measures.”Instock Goal” < .7 THEN

    '<table><tr><td style="padding-left:0" width=' || CAST(Measures.”Instock Goal” AS
    VARCHAR(20)) || ' bgcolor=#7F00FF height=16> <table><tr><td width=' ||
    CAST(Measures.”Instock” AS VARCHAR(20)) || ' bgcolor=#FFFF7E height=12>
    </td></tr></table> </td><td class=oc>' || CAST(Measures.”Instock Goal” AS
    VARCHAR(20)) || '</td></tr></table>'

ELSE

    '<table><tr><td style="padding-left:0" width=' || CAST(Measures.”Instock Goal” AS
    VARCHAR(20)) || ' bgcolor=#7F00FF height=16> <table><tr><td width=' ||
    CAST(Measures.”Instock” AS VARCHAR(20)) || ' bgcolor=#76EE00 height=12>
    </td></tr></table> </td><td class=oc>' || CAST(Measures.”Instock Goal” AS
    VARCHAR(20)) || '</td></tr></table>'

END
```

Chapter 6: Dashboards

In the previous chapters, we discussed table views, pivot table views, chart views, and other view objects. These components are assembled together to form reports (a.k.a. requests). Continuing this progression, we will now go over dashboards, which represent the outermost level of data grouping available in the Oracle BI environment. Dashboards are divided into pages (tabs) and sections consisting of related reports, prompts, and other functional/informational components. Like each of these individual pieces, dashboards as a whole possess their own set of special features and best practices. We will begin with an exploration of dashboard settings, and will continue on to explain how to use some of the additional features available for the dashboard design.

Dashboard Editor Settings

The properties and settings of a dashboard are defined in the Dashboard Editor. Here, the user can create the dashboard layout by assembling the components, arranging the content, and setting the display options.

Best Practices

BP 6.1: *When displaying a report on a dashboard, the report title should go in the dashboard section heading instead of displaying a title object within the report.*

Displaying the report title as the section heading instead of displaying the title object enables the user to collapse and expand the contents of each report/section without losing the report title (collapsing a section hides the section's content but leaves the blue bar and report title visible; this allows all of the lower page elements to move up on the screen). This will also conserve valuable real estate on your dashboard page by eliminating the extra space needed for the title. Figure 6.1 shows how sections can be collapsed within a dashboard. The top two sections have been collapsed, but the section titles remain displayed.

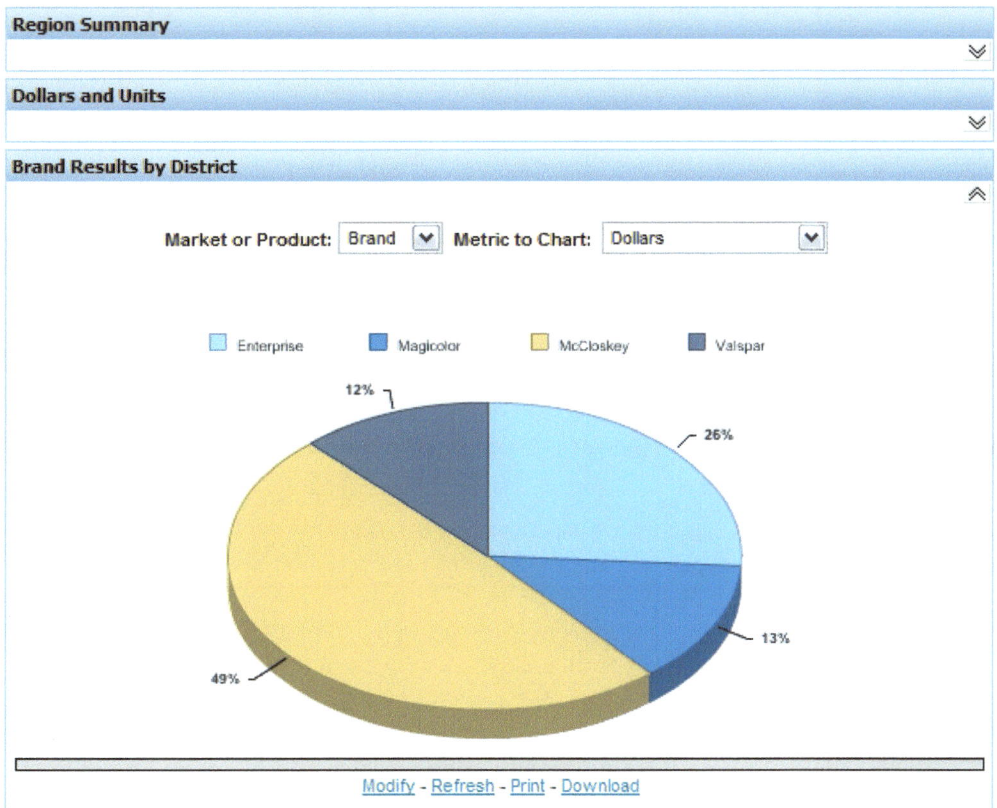

Figure 6.1 Dashboard with the first two sections collapsed.

BP 6.2: *Every attempt should be made to prevent horizontal scrolling (left to right) when viewing a dashboard; vertical scrolling (up and down) should be limited to 2 – 3 screens.*

To estimate when a dashboard page is getting too long, use the PDF option to print the page. If printing results in more than three to four pages, the dashboard is probably too long. As we mentioned in BP 5.1, keep the minimum screen resolution of the users in mind when determining if a dashboard is too wide or tall. There are many ways to reduce the height and width of a dashboard page. The following are a few of the options; the first three have already been discussed in previous chapters:

- If the report contains a large number of columns, try dividing it into smaller chunks by utilizing additional views.
- Use a view selector and/or column selector to further reduce the amount of data displayed at once
- If the report cannot be broken down into smaller chunks, consider removing the report from the dashboard altogether; instead, the report can be accessed in a separate screen via a hyperlink or directory listing.
- Reduce the section padding and column padding within the dashboard layout

BP 6.3: *A dashboard should contain a manageable number of dashboard pages (tabs), and in no case, should the tabs extend off the edge of the screen.*

While there can be no absolute rule regarding the number of acceptable dashboard pages within a dashboard, care should be given to make sure that dashboard page "creep" doesn't occur. Be deliberate with each dashboard page you create and recognize that too many pages can make it difficult for users to find what they want on the dashboard.

BP 6.4: *When using a dashboard prompt, the prompt should have its own column and section at the top of the dashboard layout, and the column width should be set to 100%.*

There are exceptions to this, such as when a single report commands its own dashboard prompt, but as a general rule of thumb, the top block of most dashboards should be reserved for a dashboard prompt.

BP 6.5: *In the Dashboard Editor, columns in the same row should be set to the same width (expressed as a percentage), unless there are specific reasons to the make the columns different sizes.*

The Dashboard Editor allows users to create a page layout with multiple rows, each of which can contain a different number of columns. Each column has a set of column properties, which can be accessed by clicking the "Properties" button in the upper right-hand corner of the column. For rows containing only one column, such as the row containing the prompt, the column width should be set to 100%. In rows containing more than one column, the total width should be divided evenly amongst all the columns (unless there are specific reasons to make the columns different sizes). For example, in a row containing two columns side by side, each column width should be set to 50%. The user must set these widths explicitly as the columns will not necessarily display equally by default.

__BP 6.6__: In the Dashboard Editor, column breaks should be accompanied by page breaks when dashboards are to be exported to PDF files.

The standard is to add page breaks within the Dashboard Editor, such that reports may be printed in their entirety on a single page, whenever possible. Note that the page break is only meaningful when the user exports the dashboard to PDF.

Quick Reference Instructions

This section contains instructions for the following topics:

- How to rename and display a Dashboard section
- How to set the width of a Dashboard column
- How to set the Section Padding and Column Padding within the Dashboard Layout
- How to add page breaks to the Dashboard

I. How to rename a Dashboard section and display the section heading

1. In the **Dashboard Editor**, click the **Rename** button in the section that will be edited
2. Enter a new section name in the text box
3. Check the **Display Section Heading** checkbox
4. Click **OK**

II. How to set the width of a Dashboard column

1. In the **Dashboard Editor**, click the **Properties** button in the column that will be edited
2. Select **Format Section** from the drop-down menu
3. Click the plus sign to expand the **Additional Formatting Options**
4. Enter a number in the text box next to **Width** (include a percent sign after the number to set the width as a percentage of the available width; if there is no percent sign, the width will be set in pixels)
5. Click **OK**

III. How to set the Column Padding and Section Padding within the Dashboard Layout

1. In the **Dashboard Editor**, click the **Properties** button in the column/section that will be edited

2. Select **Column Properties/Format Section** from the drop-down menu
3. Click the plus sign to expand the **Additional Formatting Options**
4. Enter the desired numbers for **Left Padding, Right Padding, Top Padding, Bottom Padding** (enter numbers only; do not include the percent sign)
5. Click **OK**

IV. How to add page breaks to the Dashboard

1. In the **Dashboard Editor,** click the **Properties** button in the column that is positioned just after the point where the page break will be inserted
2. Select **Break** from the drop-down menu
3. Select **Page Break** with **Column Break**
4. Click **OK**

Headers and Footers

When printing dashboards and reports, it's often necessary to include vital information regarding the reports in the headers and footers. For instance, if an executive is analyzing a hardcopy of a financial report displaying current month to date totals, he or she must know for certain when the report was run in order to utilize the information in an effective manner. If he or she believes an older report represents current data, you can probably imagine some of the problems this could potentially cause. Headers and footers also can include less pertinent items that either assist the user or simply add to the presentation value of the dashboard such as page numbers and logos. In this section, we briefly describe some of the options made available to designers within Oracle Business Intelligence. Our quick reference section will provide steps on how to add and edit dashboard headers and footers. Detailed instruction regarding specific variables and formatting options falls outside the scope of this guide. Users will need to consult the Oracle BI documentation manual for further information regarding headers and footers.

Best Practices

***BP 6.7**: Headers and footers should be configured for dashboards.*

Dashboard headers and footers can be modified from the Dashboard Editor page. These will automatically be rendered when a Dashboard page is exported to PDF via the Print to PDF feature. Basic tags such as bold, italic, underline and line break are supported within this dialog. In addition, users can insert reserved system variables such as Saved Name, Author Name, Date, Time, Page Number and Images directly into the various header/footer textboxes. Figure 6.2 on the following page shows how custom headers and footers can be enabled and configured. Notice there is also an option to expose the headers/footers within the online dashboards via the "Display in browser when applicable" option by using the checkbox.

Headers & footers can also be applied at the individual report level from within the Compound Layout view. This will enable a header/footer if the end user decides to Print to PDF from the Print link under an individual report or from within the Print Preview dialog.

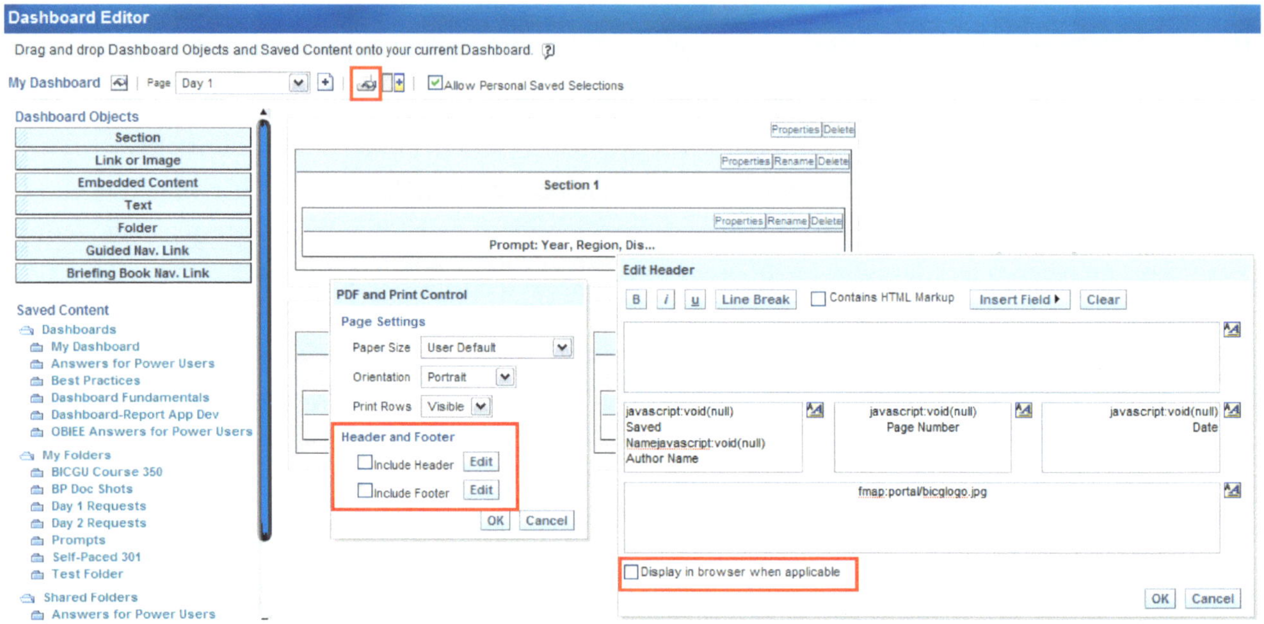

Figure 6.2 Settings for custom Headers and Footers.

Quick Reference Instructions

This section contains instructions for the following topic:

I. <u>How to add and configure the header and footer for a printed dashboard</u>

1. From the **Dashboard Editor**, click the **PDF and Print Control Properties** icon
2. Check the boxes next to **Include Header and Include Footer**
3. Click the E**dit** button to the right of either **Header** or **Footer**
4. Add desired variables and content into appropriate header or footer cells.

*See Oracle BI documentation for more detailed information on header and footer configuration

Guided Navigation

Although OBIEE uses the word "navigation" when describing three different types of functionality, in this case we are concerned with the guided navigation that allows us to display or hide a section within a dashboard. This technique can come in handy when you have specific dashboard sections and reports which you would like to keep hidden unless certain criteria are met.

Best Practices

BP 6.8*: For reports that lend themselves to showing only exceptions, guided navigation should be used to display the section as an "alert" report within a dashboard whenever certain criteria are met, and hide the section completely when they are not.*

Market	Dollars	Year Ago Dollars	% Chg Year Ago Dollars	Rank
WASHINGTON D.C.	$8,912,749	$7,416,173	20% ▲	1
COLUMBUS	$3,528,277	$3,027,835	17% ▲	2
OKLAHOMA CITY/TULSA	$2,389,214	$2,103,782	14% ▲	3
HARTFORD/NEW HAVEN	$8,177,640	$7,262,962	13% ▲	4
SAN DIEGO	$5,621,012	$5,016,404	12% ▲	5
NEW ORLEANS/MOBILE	$4,424,457	$3,949,671	12% ▲	6
SALT LAKE CITY/BOISE	$3,369,534	$3,022,901	11% ▲	7
ST. LOUIS	$5,593,864	$5,023,396	11% ▲	8
ORLANDO	$3,900,782	$3,503,515	11% ▲	9
CHICAGO	$20,082,035	$18,041,396	11% ▲	10

Figure 6.3 Dashboard section with a red heading to indicate exceptions.

As shown in Figure 6.3, one of the dashboard's sections shows a red heading, indicating that significant exceptions exist on the report it contains, even though those exceptions are not readily apparent (in this case, the tabular report only shows ten rows at a time, so the exceptions are buried further down on the page).

The user can expand the report by clicking the right navigational button with the asterisk, which will show the markets with the negative growth; these rows were hidden and could have been overlooked by the user.

Exceptions! Top and Bottom Performers

Column to be Ranked: Market

Market	Dollars	Year Ago Dollars	% Chg Year Ago Dollars	Rank
WASHINGTON D.C.	$8,912,749	$7,416,173	20% ▲	1
COLUMBUS	$3,528,277	$3,027,835	17% ▲	2
OKLAHOMA CITY/TULSA	$2,389,214	$2,103,782	14% ▲	3
HARTFORD/NEW HAVEN	$8,177,640	$7,262,962	13% ▲	4
SAN DIEGO	$5,621,012	$5,016,404	12% ▲	5
NEW ORLEANS/MOBILE	$4,424,457	$3,949,671	12% ▲	6
SALT LAKE CITY/BOISE	$3,369,534	$3,022,901	11% ▲	7
ST. LOUIS	$5,593,864	$5,023,396	11% ▲	8
ORLANDO	$3,900,782	$3,503,515	11% ▲	9
CHICAGO	$20,082,035	$18,041,396	11% ▲	10
BIRMINGHAM	$2,625,099	$2,358,894	11% ▲	11
DENVER	$10,070,137	$9,050,566	11% ▲	12
LOS ANGELES	$42,230,060	$37,994,609	11% ▲	13
NEW YORK	$46,497,637	$41,870,915	11% ▲	14
JACKSONVILLE	$1,944,671	$1,760,282	10% ▲	15
NASHVILLE	$2,410,374	$2,185,986	10% ▲	16
CLEVELAND	$12,429,258	$11,275,045	10% ▲	17
PHILADELPHIA	$29,827,430	$27,088,744	10% ▲	18
CINCINNATI	$4,232,015	$3,843,821	10% ▲	19
DETROIT	$16,404,481	$14,909,551	10% ▲	20
DALLAS	$9,370,939	$8,536,162	10% ▼	21
TAMPA	$11,292,240	$10,308,073	10% ▼	22
HOUSTON	$9,789,715	$8,942,752	9% ▼	23
PITTSBURGH	$8,884,470	$8,117,356	9% ▼	24
RALEIGH/DURHAM	$4,057,621	$3,707,757	9% ▼	25
PORTLAND	$6,854,027	$6,263,558	9% ▼	26
INDIANAPOLIS	$5,710,862	$5,220,103	9% ▼	27
ATLANTA	$7,943,643	$7,271,262	9% ▼	28
BOSTON	$25,472,468	$23,422,345	9% ▼	29
SEATTLE	$10,755,208	$9,910,527	9% ▼	30
PHOENIX	$8,256,423	$7,610,873	8% ▼	31
SAN FRANCISCO	$15,619,014	$14,410,163	8% ▼	32
KANSAS CITY	$3,688,422	$3,413,459	8% ▼	33
MINNEAPOLIS	$4,895,107	$4,550,657	8% ▼	34
MIAMI	$16,101,676	$14,973,174	8% ▼	35
MILWAUKEE	$5,121,150	$4,798,184	7% ▼	36

Records 1 - 36 (All Records)

Modify - Refresh - Print - Download

Figure 6.4 Expanded table showing all rows.

Guided navigation (or hiding or displaying sections) is fairly easy to set up, but it does require that an "exceptions" report be built to serve as the catalyst for the process (in certain instances, the main report and the exception report can be the same thing). For our example, we are going to create a report identical to the one in Figure 6.4, except it will filter out any rows where "% Chg Year Ago Dollars" is positive, that is, it will return only rows that have negative growth. If that exceptions report returns rows, we will display the section with the red heading above; otherwise we will display another section with the same report, but without the red heading.

The first step is to build the exceptions report. This can be done quickly by saving the existing report under a different name and adding a filter to the report such that the only rows returned are negative values in the "% Chg Year Ago Dollars" column. You will also notice that we have maintained the "prompted" fields, so if the user filters the dashboard content down by region, market, brand or year selections, the exceptions report will rerun, and the guided navigation will make a new determination to decide which section should show up – the one that has red title, or the one that doesn't. The report layout is shown below.

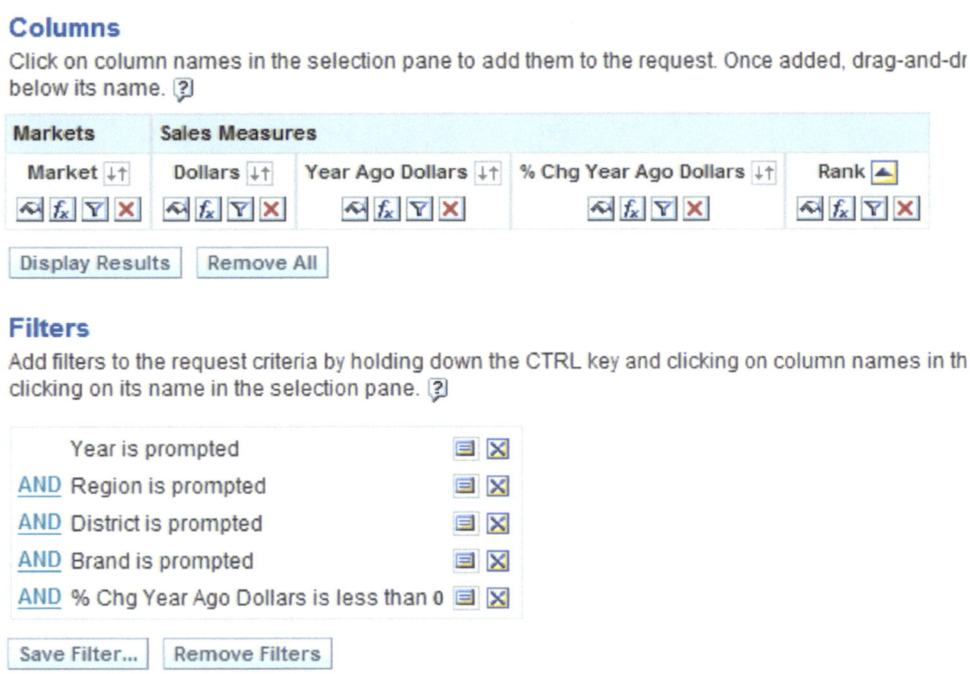

Figure 6.5 Filter settings for the Exception Report.

Within the Dashboard Editor, add two sections, and place the "Exceptions" ranking report in the top section and the original report in the bottom section. We have named the section heading on the top section "Exceptions: Top and Bottom Performers" and we have named the second section "Top and Bottom Performers". We have also changed the color of the title of the section heading for the top section to red by clicking the format icon (the two "A"s).

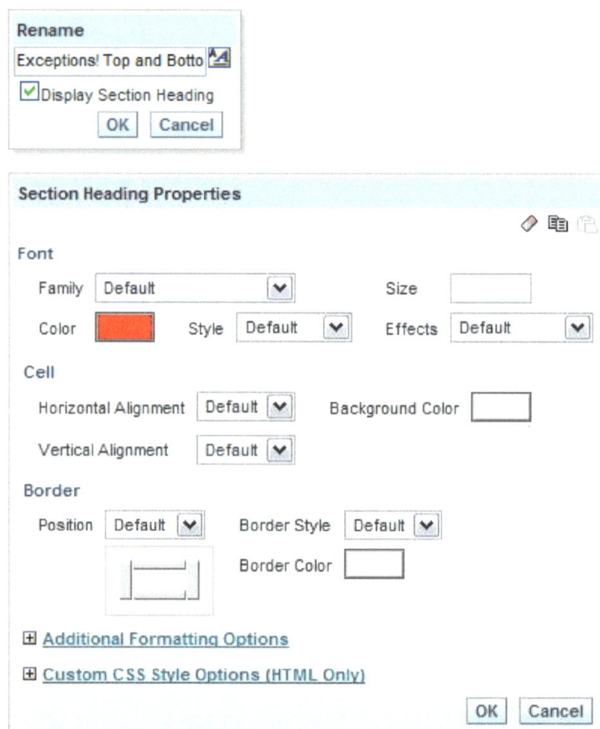

Figure 6.6 Section heading properties for the exceptions report.

To enable the section hiding or displaying, click on the "Properties" option on the section, and select "Guided Navigation". The dialog box below will appear. Using the browse button, select the exceptions report that you just created, and select the radio button to show the section "If request returns rows". This will cause this section to display if the exception report returns rows, namely any row with a decline from the previous year.

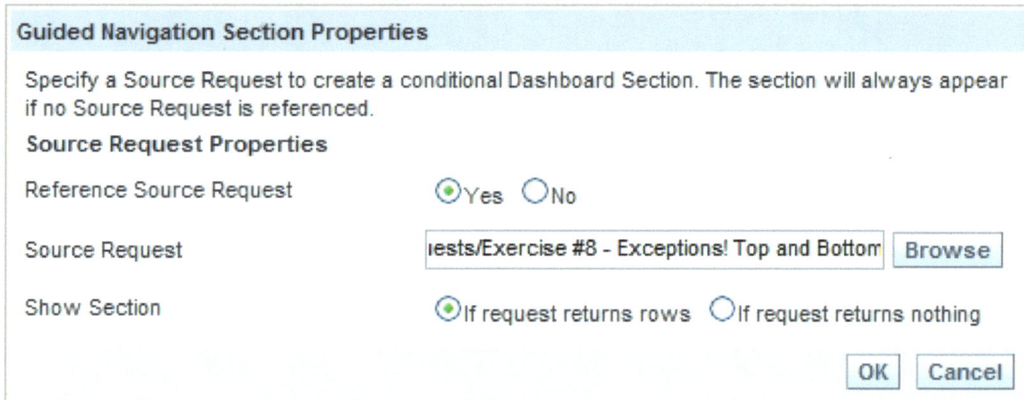

Figure 6.7 Guided navigation settings for when there are exceptions.

Repeat this process for the next section, once again choosing the exceptions report for the source request, but change the setting of the radio button to show the section "If request returns nothing".

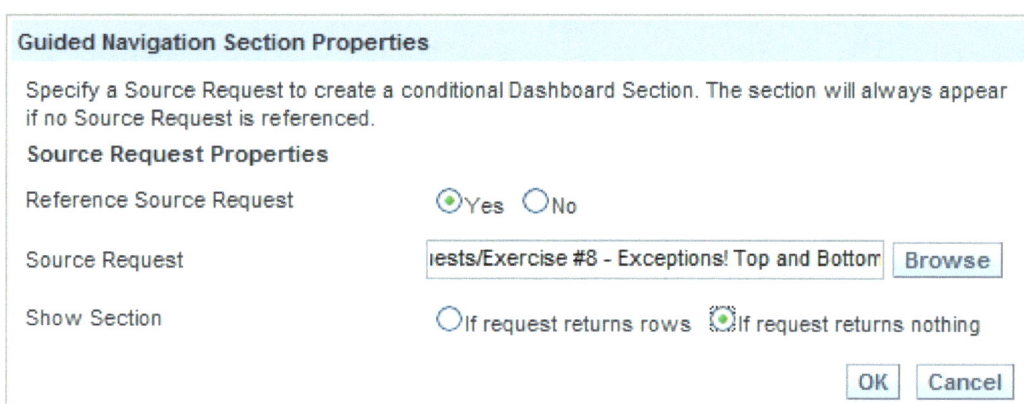

Figure 6.8 Guided navigation settings for when there are no exceptions.

When a user accesses this dashboard from this moment further, OBIEE will run the exceptions report first to determine which dashboard section to display.

Bonus feature:

An additional way that we can take advantage of this function is to hide *all* dashboard sections until selections have been made in dashboard prompt. This is important when the contents of a dashboard are only meaningful after a selection has been made (for example, on a "Customer Detail" dashboard which is only meaningful after a customer name or ID has been selected, and is not meaningful if multiple customer names or IDs are selected) and for when a default selection does not make sense. The "Exceptions Report" that can drive the appearance or disappearance of all sections can be based on a report that counts the number of rows returned, and is only "True" when a single row is returned. For example, the report below with its calculation (performing a count of districts) and its filter (returning no rows unless the count of districts is exactly one) and its prompted field (accepting a prompt for district) can be used to hide all sections on a dashboard until a district has been selected from a prompt, and the "Go" button has been clicked.

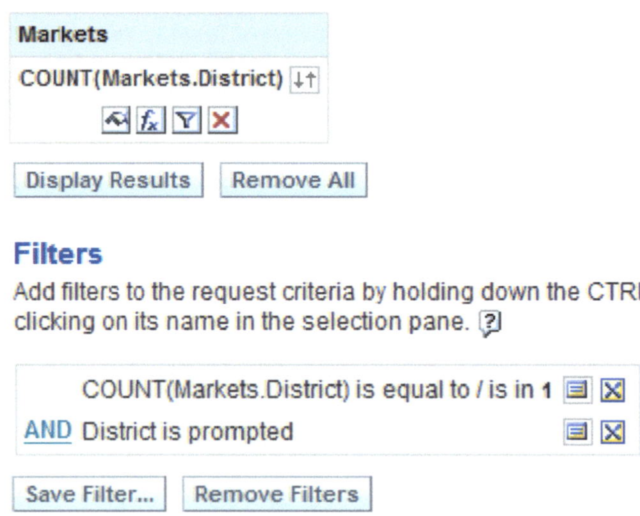

Figure 6.9 Settings for a "dummy" report used to display dashboard sections only after a prompt selection has been made.

Using the "Exceptions" report in Figure 6.9, we can construct a dashboard similar to the one in Figure 6.10, which has no visible sections until a district is selected from the prompt.

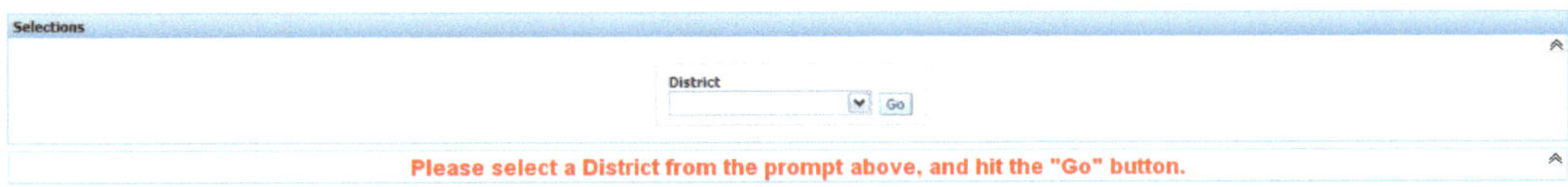

Figure 6.10 Dashboard with all sections hidden.

Once a District is selected and the "Go" button is hit, the hidden sections appear as in Figure 6.11, with reports that have been filtered by the prompt selection.

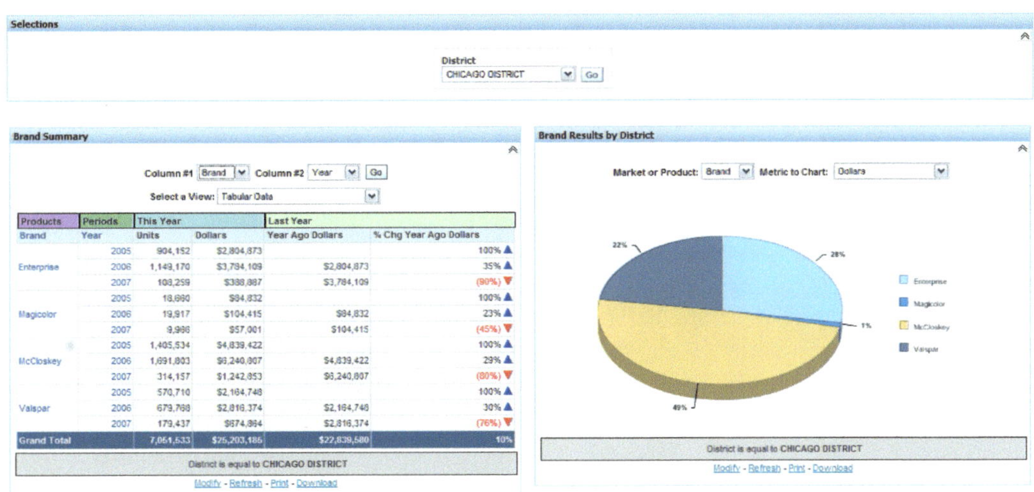

Figure 6.11 Dashboard showing sections after a prompt selection has been made.

The construction of this dashboard was done similar to the process described above. The two sections that contain reports have their guided navigation properties set so that they do not show unless the exceptions report returns rows (that is, when only one district has been selected).

Finally, an additional section is added with a text object that explains how to use this page. This new section contains simple HTML as shown in Figure 6.12, and its section is set with the opposite properties. In other words, it should only be displayed when the exception report returns no rows (when no districts or more than one have been selected).

It should be noted that this clever dashboard arrangement does not come without its limits. If too many sections require guided navigation reports to run first before OBIEE can determine whether to display them or not, there could be a performance bottleneck and OBIEE will not be able to make this determination quickly. When this happens it is very obvious to the user and does not make for a good user experience, so care should be taken to make sure this doesn't happen.

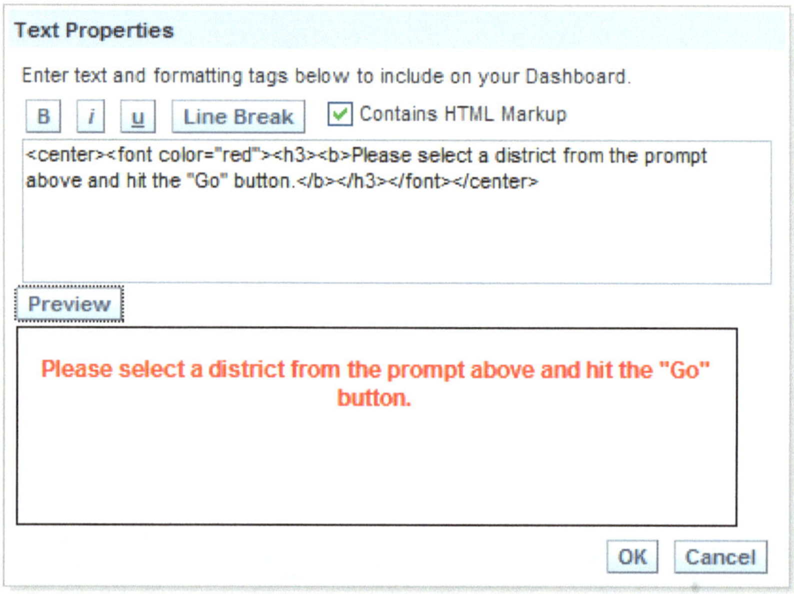

Figure 6.12 HTML used to create a dashboard section containing instructions.

Chapter 7: Tips and Tricks

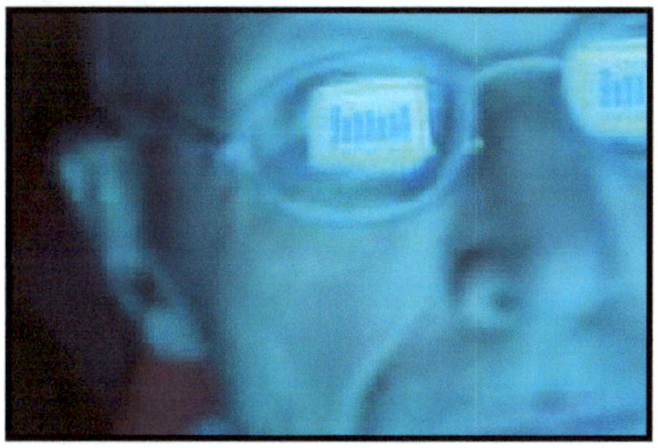

BI Consulting Group's custom, itererative methodology is, in part, enabled by our wide use of simple short cuts and other "tricks" to minimize the amount of time required to create powerful Dashboards and reports. Of all the chapters in this guide, this one may end up saving you the most time and effort in your Dashboard and report development.

Tips and Tricks

***Tip 7.1**: You can use existing charts and pivot tables to create additional views, instead of starting over from scratch.*

Once you have developed a chart or pivot table view that meets all of your best practice standards, you can easily reuse the view as a template to create other similar views rather than duplicating efforts by creating the new views from scratch. The trick is to create a duplicate copy of the existing view and then modify the copy. There is a "Duplicate View" option in the editing mode for charts and pivot tables.

Using this option will automatically create a new sequentially numbered version of the current view. For example, if you duplicate a chart view, a new chart view will be created with the name "Chart: 2". Duplicating views is especially useful when you want to display the same data using two different types of charts, such as a pie chart and a line bar combo chart. Using this technique, in just a few minutes you can produce multiple charted analyses of the same data elements, each of which can be added to a view selector.

***Tip 7.2**: You can use an existing report to create additional reports, instead of starting over from scratch.*

Reports can be copied and transformed much in the same way as views. Once a successful report has been developed using best practices, it makes sense to recycle as much of the development as possible when creating the next report. This is particularly true when reports have very similar analytic requirements, but might vary by a few metrics or attributes.

For example, if the requirements for a dashboard page stipulate that analysis be performed to show the sales performance by sales organization as well as product line, both sets of reports do not need to be developed from scratch. We can use a "highlight and replace" technique to cut hours off of development.

As an example, the report definition in Figure 7.1 contains three charts, one pivot table, and one tabular view, all of which were formatted to meet the standards outlined in this guide. The report also contains a column selector and a filter.

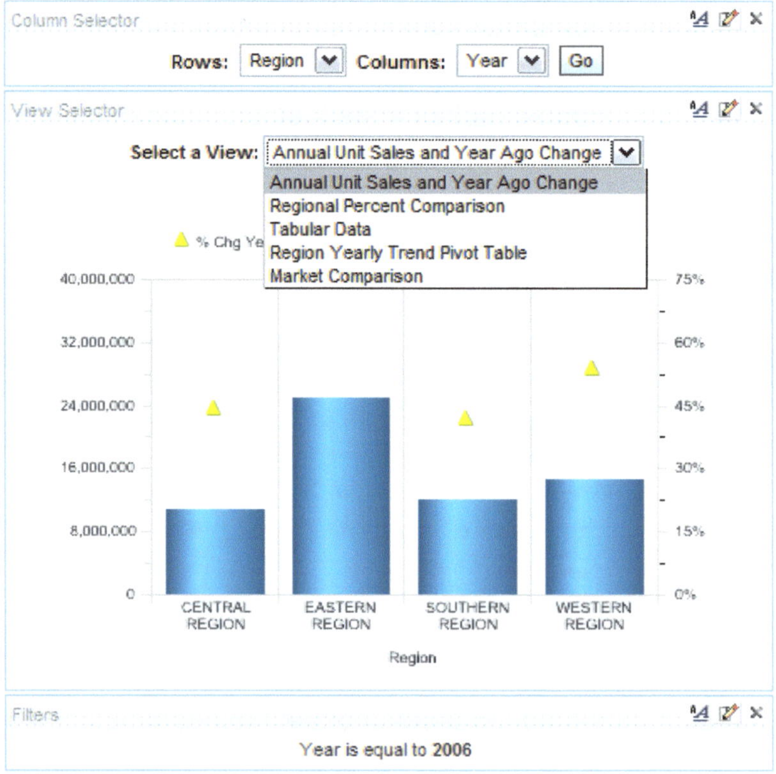

Figure 7.1 Example report containing multiple views.

To create an identically structured report that substitutes brand for region would be time consuming to say the least, so here's the shortcut:

Go to the *Criteria* tab, and click on the Calculation icon on any column that should be dropped and replaced. In this case, we will click on the Edit Formula button in the region column, which would open up the dialog box in Figure 7.2. Highlight all the text in the Column Formula text box (in this case, the text formula is "Markets.Region").

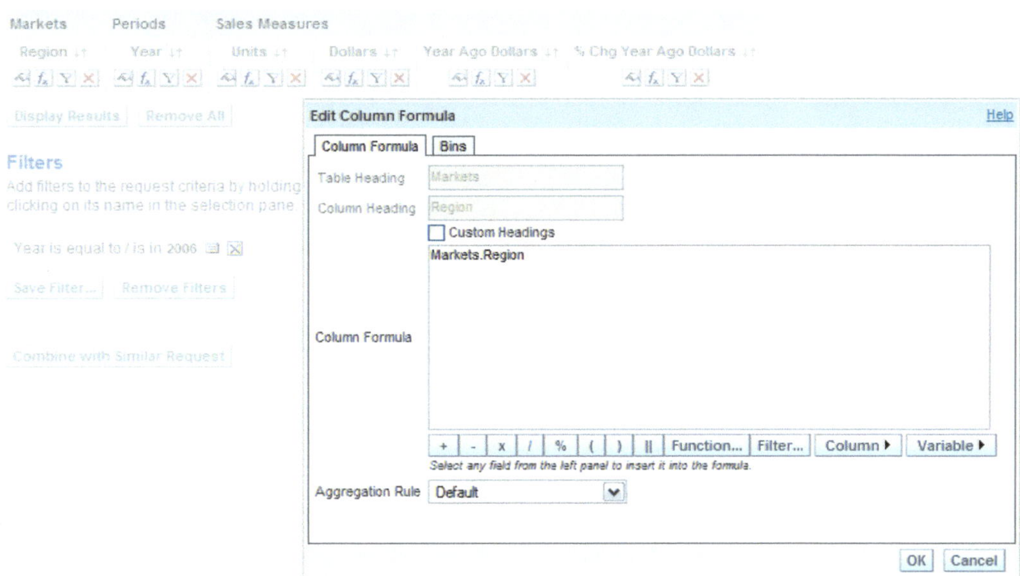

Figure 7.2 Edit Column Formula dialog box

From the Pick List on the left side of Answers, pick the column that you would like to use to replace regions. In this case, we will select the "Brand" column.

You might notice that even though "Products.Brand" has now replaced "Markets.Region", the column and table headings still reflect the old attribute, "Region". Do not worry; these headings will be fixed automatically. Click the OK button and you will see that the column name has been appropriately updated to show the new column name as in Figure 7.3. Save the report under a new name, and you suddenly have a five-view product analysis report that follows every standard and was built in about 30 seconds.

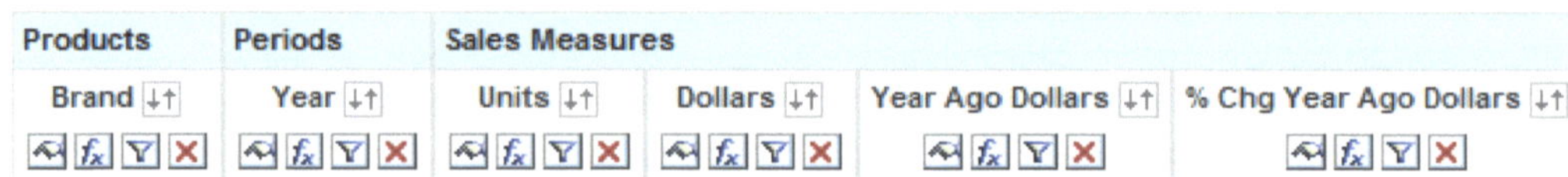

Figure 7.3 Updated criteria for the replaced column.

NOTE: Dropping a column (by clicking its "X") and adding a new column will NOT have the same effect as above. That process will break charts and pivot tables, and will require you to re-edit each of those objects to use the new column.

Once you have finished replacing columns, run the report and test all of its features, including all views. You may need to rename certain views (in our example, the word "Region" still appears in several of the views; these references should be replaced with the word "Brand").

Tip 7.3: *Use copy and paste to quickly add the report name to the dashboard section heading.*

As discussed in the Dashboard Editor section, one of our best practices is to remove the title from the report, and to put each report into its own section, with the report title being added to the section heading. To quickly do this without retyping the report title into the section heading, click the Rename button on the report object (in Figure 7.4 we clicked the Rename button on the "Brand Summary" report). Highlight the name and press CTRL+C to copy the name. Close that box, and click the Rename button on the section. Highlight the default name (in this case, it says "Section 2"). Press CTRL-V to paste the report name into the section heading, and click OK.

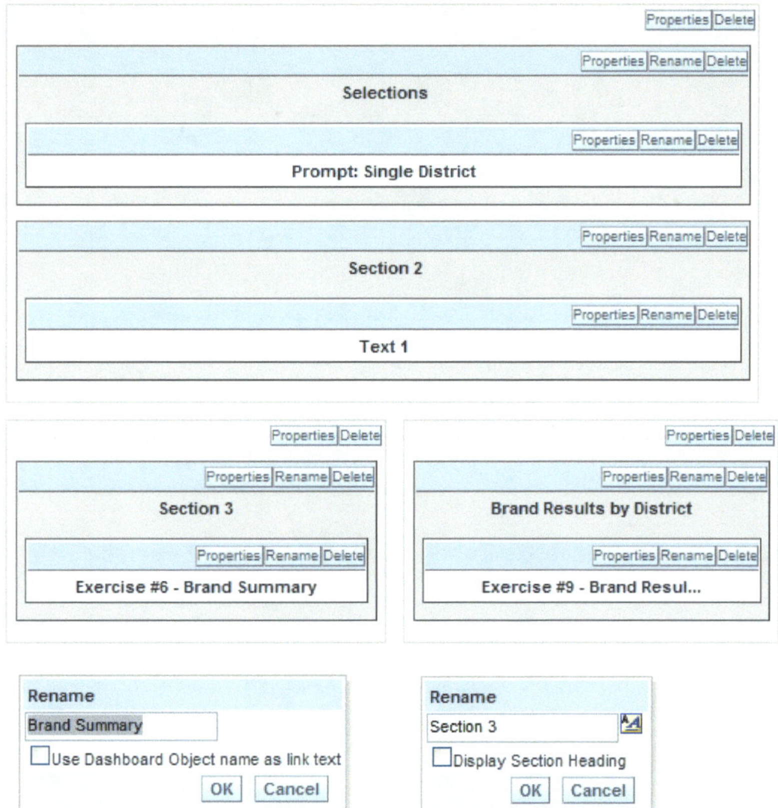

Figure 7.4 These are the 3 screens involved in renaming the Dashboard section.

***Tip 7.4**: When viewing a dashboard, if you need to edit a report, avoid using the Modify link below the report; instead you should use the Modify Request option in the Dashboard Editor.*

When you are about to modify a report that has already been placed in a dashboard, rather than clicking the "Modify" link under that report, go to the Dashboard Editor, and select the "Modify Request" option from the Properties menu instead. Using the Modify link on the dashboard screen could result in inadvertently saving the prompt settings or drill downs that occurred while the report was displayed on the dashboard. The "Modify" link was designed for users with Answers access who can't overwrite the report on the dashboard, not developers who can.

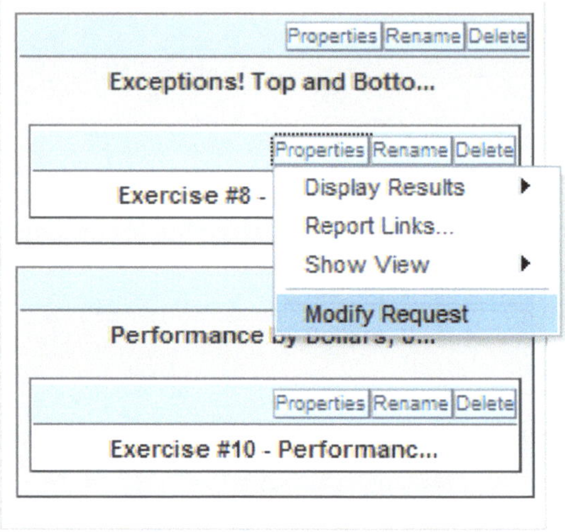

Figure 7.5 Modify Request link accessed from the Properties menu.

***Tip 7.5**: When viewing a dashboard, use the "Dashboard" link at the top of the page to refresh the dashboard (a refresh will reset all column selectors, view selectors, and drill-downs back to their original states).*

***Tip 7.6**: When testing report functionality in Answers (such as drill-downs, navigation, column selectors, view selectors, etc.) use the "Preview" mode instead of testing within the compound layout / design mode.*

Any changes that occur to the report in Preview mode will not affect the underlying report definition. On the other hand, if you drill down on a chart (for example) in the chart editor or compound layout, your entire report definition (including the filters and criteria) will be changed to reflect the new drilled-down level.

***Tip 7.7:** Use the CTRL key while selecting a column from the pick list if you need to create a filter based on that column, but do not wish to include the column in the report.*

If you would like to add a filter to a report, but do not want to have the filter column displayed within the report itself, it is not necessary to add the column to the report, create a filter, and then delete the column from the report. Instead, hold the CTRL key down when clicking the attribute from the pick list. This will automatically open the Create/Edit Filter dialog box without adding the column to the report.

Quick Reference Instructions

This section contains instructions for the following topics:

- How to duplicate an existing view to create a new one
- How to replace columns in an existing report to create a new one
- How to modify a report from a dashboard
- How to copy and paste a report name into a dashboard section heading
- How to create a filter for a column that is not in the request

I. How to duplicate an existing view to create a new one

1. In the **Results** tab, open the view that will be duplicated
2. Click the icon to the right of the drop-down view menu; this icon's tool tip reads "Duplicate, specialize, or delete the current view"
3. In the pop-up menu, select the **Duplicate View** option

II. How to replace columns in an existing report to create a new one

1. Open the **Criteria** tab of the existing report
2. Click the **Edit Formula** button of the column that will be replaced
3. Delete all of the text in the **Column Formula** text box
4. Insert the column formula for the new column by clicking on the new column's name in the pick list on the left side of the screen
5. Click **OK**
6. Repeat steps 2-5 for any other columns that need to be replaced
7. Click the **Save Request** button on the right-hand side of the screen
8. Save the new request under a different name than the original request

Note: It is not necessary to change column headings or table headings of the replacement columns; these headings will be changed automatically. However, it *is* necessary to change any other text in the new report that still references the replaced columns.

III. How to modify a report from a dashboard

1. From the **Dashboard** screen, click the **Page Options** drop-down menu
2. Select the **Edit Dashboard** option
3. Click the **Properties** button of the report that will be modified
4. Select the **Modify** option in the **Properties** drop-down menu

IV. How to copy and paste a report name into a dashboard section heading

1. In the **Dashboard Editor**, click the **Rename** button in the report whose name will be used to rename the parent section
2. In the **Rename** dialog box, highlight the report name
3. Copy the report name by using the keyboard shortcut **CTRL + C** or by right clicking on the highlighted text and selecting the **Copy** option from the pop-up menu
4. Click **Cancel** in the **Rename** dialog box
5. In the **Dashboard Editor**, click the **Rename** button in the **section** that will be renamed
6. In the **Rename** dialog box, highlight the section name
7. Paste the copied report name into the text box by using the keyboard shortcut **CTRL + V** or by right clicking on the highlighted text and selecting the **Paste** option from the pop-up menu
8. Click **OK**

V. How to create a filter for a column that is not in the request

1. In the **Results** tab, hold down the **CTRL** key and click on the column name in the pick list on the left side of the screen
2. In the **Create/Edit Filter** dialog box, enter the filter criteria and click **OK**; the filter criteria will be applied to the report, but the column will not be added.

Chapter 8: Naming Conventions & Data Format

Our last section on naming conventions and data formats is the one subject that will change the most from customer to customer. Our intent is to identify a set of standards where none exist, not to supercede established standards that are already in place. If your organization has not already decided upon a set of rules to govern the wording and formatting of names and data regarding your dashboards and reports, you may want to take some of the standards outlined below into consideration.

Naming Conventions

Standard naming conventions should be established for reports and other objects. Failing to do so may not cause immediate problems, but may create quite a few headaches down the road. When naming reports, you should strive to give your users a good idea of what they'll find in the report simply by reading the name. The organization and names of folders and dashboards should also be agreed upon and understood by everyone who's been granted access. When multiple designers are creating and saving folders, requests, and other objects within the same directory, it's crucial that guidelines have been set with regards to names as well as folder structure. In the Best Practices section, we've offered some tips that should bring you closer to your goal of getting everyone on the same page with regards to your dashboards and reports.

Best Practices

***BP 8.1**: Report names should be concise, descriptive, and fit into a single display row when placed in a dashboard or when used as a section title.*

***BP 8.2**: Report titles should include three key ingredients when applicable, which are the role for which the report is intended, how the report is filtered and aggregated, and the key measures included.*

We consider including the key measures in the report title to be the minimum requirement for report names, but you will find in most cases that the other two items will apply as well. Other creative names may be used that are meaningful to the business as long as the other naming standards are followed. Also, the first letter of each primary word should generally be capitalized. The following are examples of report titles that apply the above best practices for naming reports:

- "Regional Managers Top Ten Stores by Percent to Plan"
- "Stores with at least 90 Day Decline in Customer Satisfaction"
- "Four Week Trend of Discounting for Regional Managers"

Note that in the second example above, this report is not specific to any role, and could be used by multiple roles including management, finance, marketing, etc. This will tend to be the norm since the data displayed within each report can be driven by data rights at the individual and role level, such that the "Stores with at least 90 Day Decline in Customer Satisfaction" report would be a "Regional Manager" report when accessed by a regional manager; and a "Corporate" report when accessed by someone with corporate data security rights, etc.

***BP 8.3**: If you use the Title view, the name used to save the report should be set as the title displayed when the report is executed.*

It can be confusing for everyone when a report is referred to by multiple names. Keeping the saved report name and the report title consistent will help to avoid this confusion and will make it much easier for users and designers to discuss reports.

A couple of additional options for report titles which we haven't made best practices, but may prove to be useful for you are listed below:

- If your chart or table is drillable, a subtitle such as "(Drill on chart for details)" may be added to provide the user with information about the report's function.

- You may wish to display the run time of each report. If this standard is followed, it should be consistent across all production reports.

BP 8.4*: Create shared folders structures using two major groupings; user roles and subject areas (or dashboards).*

Either convention is acceptable, but should be determined by the number of reports within subject area or roles that are shared. The most useful convention is to group common reports into subject area folders only; and group role-specific reports into subject area folders first, and role folders second. In most cases, directory structures will have approximately two-to-three levels of folders.

Examples include:

- Shared/Sales/Stores with at least 90 Day Decline in Customer Satisfaction
- Shared/Sales/Regional Managers/Top Ten Stores by Percent to Plan

BP 8.5*: All prompt names should begin with the word "Prompt:" which should be followed by an abbreviated list of the attributes included in the prompt.*

Following the above practice can save designers from plenty of frustration due to the fact that many reports and prompts will have very similar names. For instance, the name "Prompt: Year, Region, Store" is short and to the point and there's virtually no chance of misinterpretation. As you'll read below, you also may want to create a special folder that contains only prompts to avoid confusion.

BP 8.6*: All alerts should be preceded by the word "Alert:" and use similar naming conventions to reports.*

BP 8.7*: All filters should be preceded by the word "Filter:" and use similar naming conventions to reports.*

These two guidelines borrow from some of the previously mentioned best practices for reports and prompts. Using this convention, it's perfectly clear whether an object is a filter or alert as opposed to a report, and using the rules we've discussed for report names will help to ensure users know the precise subject matter. Below are a few examples of proper naming of alerts and filters:

- "Alert: Stores with Declining Customer Satisfaction for 6 or more weeks"
- "Filter: Stores open for at least One Year"

***BP 8.8**: Non-report objects should be placed in the same directory structure as defined for reports, and then placed in their own subfolders with names such as "Prompts" and "Alerts".*

Examples include:

- /Sales/Prompts/Prompt: Year, Region Name, Store Name
- /Sales/Regional Managers/Prompts/Prompt: Year, Store Name, Compensation Level
- /Sales/Regional Managers/Alerts/Alerts: Stores with Declining Customer Satisfaction for 6 or More Weeks

There can be exceptions to this, of course. Security will influence some of these structures, as will objects that are shared across multiple areas, such as prompts. Avoid creating multiple instances of the same prompts and filters, for example.

Data Format Standards

This section provides a standard that can be applied to the specific data found within your reports. As we've mentioned above, if your organization has already agreed upon certain guidelines to follow with regards to data formatting, then you should continue to use them. The most important aspects of data formatting are comprehension and consistency. This means that your first concern is whether your users understand the values in a certain format. If so, your next goal is to make sure the same guidelines are followed in every report you create. The settings below are the ones we recommend for maximum readability and coherence. To use this guide, open the Column Properties dialog box for a particular column and switch to the Data Format tab as we've done in Figure 8.1. Then check the Override Default Data Format checkbox and enter the settings we've provided for the appropriate data type.

Percentages

Treat Numbers As: Percentage
Negative Format: Minus: -123
Decimal Places: 1
Use 1000's Separator: Yes
Resulting format: 90.1% or -90.1%

Numbers

Treat Numbers As: Number
Negative Format: Minus: -123
Decimal Places: 0
Use 1000's Separator: Yes
Resulting format: 90 or -90

Currency

Treat Numbers As: Currency
Currency Symbol: $ Warehouse Default
Negative Format: Parentheses: (123)
Decimal Places: 2
Use 1000's Separator: Yes
Resulting format: $90.00 or ($90.00)

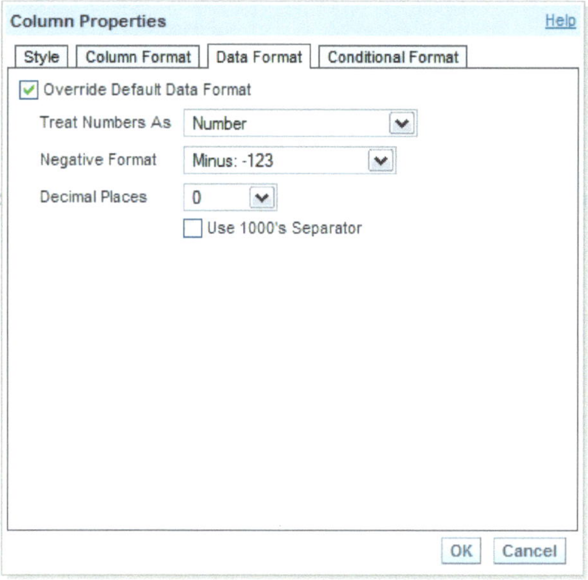

Figure 8.1 Column Properties dialog box

It is recommended that you spend the time defining the default data formats for all of your subject area columns ***before*** building any reports. This can be done in Answers by viewing multiple columns in a table view simultaneously and then methodically setting the data format for each column, one-by-one. Repeat until all columns are addressed. The process is tedious, but it will help your report developers and prevent settings like formatting from being saved as the default alongside the data format. There is nothing more annoying for a developer than to constantly use a column on reports and have to undo its default formatting.

Appendix

Quick Reference Index

Best Practice Index

Best Practices Checklist

Table Checklist

	Best Practice	Tool
1	Green-Bars Enabled (for list style tabular reports)	**Toolbar**
2	Set Report Width to 100%	**Toolbar , Additional Formatting**
3	Grand Total on Bottom of Table (unless total does not make sense), Report Based Totals Checked	**Toolbar**
4	Enable Column Sorting	**Toolbar**
5	Paging Controls at the Bottom (default)	**Toolbar**
6	Display Column & Table Headings as Separate Rows	**Toolbar**
7	Rename Parent Column with More Appropriate Name	**Column , Column Format,**
8	Add Background Colors to Table Headings (use subdued colors)	**Column , Column Format,**
9	Calculations are Best Done in the Metadata unless One of a Kind	**Column ,Column Formula**
10	The Parent Attribute is in the Left-Outer-Most Column, if you Stack Parent & Column Attributes use Pivot-Table View	

Pivot Table Checklist

	Best Practice	Tool
1	Green-Bars Enabled (for list style tabular reports, not reports with some type of grouping)	**Toolbar**
2	Set Report Width to 100%	**Mid Shaded Section**
3	Sub-Totals after Detailed Line Items & Grand Total at Bottom of Report	
4	Column Heading Display in Section Properties should be Above	**Section**
5	Check Option "Insert Page Display" (applied when printed to PDF)	**Section**

Compound View Checklist

	Best Practice	Tool
1	Title is Dropped (Title will then be "Renamed" in Dashboard)	**Title View**
2	Filter View Added (when data being filtered is not obvious from report)	**Add View:**
3	Filter View should be the Last View and be Shaded Medium Gray with a Border	**Tab, Grey 3Rd Down on Right**
4	Test Report using Preview Button Rather Than From Editor (for all reports)	

Column Selector Checklist

	Best Practice	Tool
1	Consider Column Selectors to Further Improve Analytical Capabilities	**Add View: Column Selector**
2	Add Column Selectors to Mimic Re-Pivoting a Pivot Table Within Dashboard	**Add View: Column Selector**
3	Use this Feature to Avoid Traditional Multi Column Report	**Add View: Column Selector**
4	"Uncheck" to Enable "GO" Feature when more than One Column	**Automatically Refresh …"**
5	Label Appropriately, such as "Attribute in Bars" or Metric to Compare"	
6	Consider "Top" & "Bottom" Report to Replace Ranking Using Column Selector	
7	If Used to Replace Metric in Pie Chart, only Use for Ordinal #s not %s or Indexes	

View Selector Checklist

	Best Practice	Tool
1	"Break Apart" Reports that are too Wide by Using Multiple Pivot Tables and Adding them in View Selector	**Create Multiple Pivot Tables, Add View: View Selector**
2	Use this Feature to Reduce Length of Dashboard Page	**Add View: View Selector**
3	Use on Analytical Reports to Reduce Amount of Searching for End User	**Add View: View Selector**
4	Allow at least Two Views on Each Report, include Tabular or Pivot Table View	**Add View: View Selector**
5	Caption" Select a View" to Left of View Selector or "Metric Location"	**"Caption" Within View Selector**
6	Rename View to a more Meaningful Name	**"Rename" Within View Selector**
7	Rename Tabular Views to "Detailed Data" or Tabular Data"	**"Rename" Within View Selector**

Conditional Formatting Checklist

	Best Practice	Tool
1	Tables and Pivot Tables with +/- and % Columns should Always have Red/Blue Up/Dwn Arrows to the Right of the Number (to the left of text)	**Column , Conditional Formatting Tab**
2	For Graphics (rather than background/text colors) Use the "Null" Images for Conditions that are Not Met to Maintain Alignment	
3	Include a Legend in Your Report	**Add View: Legend**

Chart Checklist

	Best Practice	Tool
1	Place Legend on Top	**, Legend Tab**
2	Remove Right & Left Labels if Metrics are Displayed in the Legend	**, Custom Title, Erase**
3	Data Labels Displayed Always when Easily Readable, Default on Rollover when > 10 Pie Wedges or > 6 Bars are Displayed	
4	For Printed Chart w/o Data Labels add Table or Pivot Table View under the Chart; or View Selector; or 2 Chart Views (one with Data Labels)	
5	Use Default Colors, Background Colors & Fonts Except when Trying to "Call Out" Part of Series	
6	Bar Charts are 2D with Cylinder Chart Type	**Type & Style**
7	Use Horizontal Chart when Data Series ≤ 6 or when Trend; Use Vertical Chart when > 6 or when Width Needs to be Narrow to Fit Dashboard	**Graph**
8	Use Duplicate View to Reuse Charted Views to Quickly Create an Alternate View for View Selector	**, Duplicate View**
9	For Pie Charts use 3D	**Graph**
10	Use Line-Bar Combo when Dissimilar Metrics	**Graph**
11	Consider Point Markers for Line-Bar Charts	**, Line Tab, Set Width to 0,**
12	Consider Bubble Chart for Insight into Interaction of Three Metrics, use Additive # for X/Y and Non-Additive #s like Avg or % for Z Axis (bubble size)	**Graph**

Dashboard Checklist

	Best Practice	Tool
1	The Prompt is in its Own Section at 100% Width, A Dashboard Prompt is Preferred over Report Prompts (Dashboard Prompts should be set to Page).	**Properties (Upper Rt. On Column), Column Properties**
2	Each Report is Dropped into its Own Section	**Click on Report & Drag**
3	Page Contains Two Columns	**Properties, Break, Column Break**
4	Each Column is at 50% Width	**Properties (Upper Rt. On Column), Column Properties**
5	Each Report is Renamed as the Title was Dropped from the Compound Layout to Save Space. Also, Allows Report to be Collapsed Leaving the Renamed Title	**Section, Rename**
6	"Display Section Heading" is Checked On	**Section, Rename**
7	Guided Navigation within a Section can be Used to Indicate Exceptions	**Section, Properties**
8	To Place Links on Report	**Report Properties, Report Links**
9	No More than 8 Tabs within Dashboard	
10	Allow Drill in Place and/or Collapsible	**Section, Properties**
11	Limit Vertical Scrolling to 2-3 Pages	**See Pg 8 of "Best Practices" for Solutions if > 3 Pages**

Presentation Layer Naming Checklist

	Best Practice	Tool
1	First Letter of Major Words are Capitalized	
2	No Underscores or Other Database Styling	
3	Only One Level of Sub-Folder is Used	
4	No more than 25 Items in a Single Folder	
5	If > 25 Items in a Major Folder list out Items used Frequently, Group Rest in a Sub-Folder	
6	Avoid Abbreviations, or Limit to Comply with #7 below	
7	<25 Letters/Spaces, Goal 15 or Less and 5 Words or Less	
8	Never use Dimension, Fact or Data in Presentation Layer naming	

Report Naming Checklist

	Best Practice	Tool
1	Short, Descriptive, and Fit into a Single Row in Dashboard or Used as Section Name	
2	3 Key Topics: Role Intended, how Filtered/Aggregated. Key Measures Contained (Minimum)	
3	Other Creative Names can be Added to the Standards	
4	First Letter of Primary Words are Capitalized	
5	Names can be Driven by Data Rights at the Individual and Role Level	
6	Report Name shall be Displayed as Report Title	
7	Sub-Title may be added for Chart or Drillable Table to provide Info @ Report's Function	
8	Standard may be included to Display Run Time & be Consistent Across all Production Reports	
9	Prompt Naming should be Preceded by the Word "Prompt"	

About BI Consulting Group

BI Consulting Group is, at the time of this publication, Oracle's largest consulting partner focused exclusively on Oracle Business Intelligence (formerly Siebel Business Analytics and nQuire). Our staff comes from companies like Siebel, Oracle, IBM, Accenture, and other large companies running Oracle Business Intelligence.

Collectively, we have more than 280 Oracle Business Intelligence projects under our belt, and 80 years of Oracle BI experience. That kind of experience isn't duplicated anywhere in the market; even at the largest consulting firms. The average experience of our staff is 3+ years working on Oracle BI implementations, and more than ten years in Business Intelligence and data warehousing. All that, and we are still 100% reference-able.

BI Consulting Group provides our clients with experienced Oracle Business Intelligence and data warehousing consultants who provide a variety of consulting services for the design, development, deployment and maintenance of Oracle BI applications. These services include project management; requirements development and application design; metadata development; report and dashboard design and development; data warehouse design and development; and ETL development for standalone implementations or implementations of Oracle's prepackaged analytic applications. Our methodology utilizes a rapid iterative model, ensuring that final deliverables provide insight, rather than just reports.

About The Authors

Amy Mayer brings more than 10 years of Business Intelligence and Data Warehouse experience to BI Consulting Group, beginning in 1998 at Schneider National and GE Capital, where she gained extensive experience in data warehouse best practices. Amy then joined Business Objects as a senior engineer, before joining Jostens in 2001 as a manager within their Business Intelligence team, where she played an integral part in Jostens' award winning implementation of Siebel Business Analytics.

Since founding BI Consulting Group, Amy has managed many of the most complex, most successful implementations of Oracle BI Enterprise Edition, anywhere in the world.

Kevin McGinley brings more than 12 years of experience in Business Intelligence and Data Warehousing, and more than 9 years of consulting experience to BI Consulting Group.

Through his experiences while leading many large data warehouse projects for several major CPG companies, Kevin has designed multiple Data Warehouse and Business Intelligence "Best Practices" that have been incorporated into BI Consulting Group's custom methodologies.

www.ingramcontent.com/pod-product-compliance
Lightning Source LLC
LaVergne TN
LVHW070954210926
848482LV00002B/209